HOUSE OF

portraits from a jerusalem neighborhood

WINDOWS

✕✕

ADINA HOFFMAN

STEERFORTH PRESS
south royalton, vermont

For information about permission to reproduce
selections from this book, write to:
Steerforth Press L.C.
P.O. Box 70, South Royalton, Vermont 05068

LIBRARY OF CONGRESS CATALOGING-IN-PUBLICATION DATA

Hoffman, Adina.
House of windows : portraits from a Jerusalem neighborhood / Adina Hoffman.
            p.   cm.
ISBN 1-58642-001-1 (alk. paper)
1. Morashah (Jerusalem) 2. Jerusalem — Description and travel. I. Title.

DS 109.8.M57 H64 2000
956.94'42—dc21
HOFFMAN   00-038798

PHOTO CREDITS
Pages 71, 193 © 2000 by Debbie Hill
Page 97 courtesy of the Central Zionist Archives
Page 131 © 2000 by D. Brauner

Grateful acknowledgment is made for permission to reprint excerpts from
Mandate Days: British Lives in Palestine 1918–1948
© 1997 by A. J. Sherman, published by Thames and Hudson, Ltd.

For Peter

"The King has presented an Etruscan vase, the most beautiful in the world, to the Museum of Naples. What a pity I cannot draw it!"

In the meantime, the housemaid has broken a kitchen teacup; let me see if you can draw one of the pieces.

John Ruskin
The Laws of Fésole

THE AERIAL COURTYARD

xxxxxxxxxxxxxxxxxxxxxxxxxxxxxxxxxxxxxxxxxxxxxxx

with its flight of worn limestone steps, its slender columns and iron banisters, rising at intervals into delicate archways, the house called to mind a host of mismatched objects and structures, the entire assortment of which might suggest, together, something of its quirky elegance, but none of which alone does justice to the building's eccentric proportions. It had the multiple, zigzagging decks of a luxury liner, the intricate balconies and catwalks of a stage set, the busy grid of a crossword puzzle, and the tall, spindly struts of an oversized canopy bed. All and none. Whatever else it resembled (as it turned out, some other thing or form almost every time I mounted the stairs), we both felt the mysterious lure of the place in excited silence the first time we ascended. It was nighttime and December. The bite of the

air made the stars appear sharper with each step upward.

E., the young architect who had just bought the apartment perched at the uppermost back corner of the building, had decided to travel from Jerusalem to Rome for nine months. He'd been offered work at an Italian firm and meant to rent his new place for a reasonable fee. Sleepy-lidded and skinny-hipped, he greeted us at the door and waved us casually inside the cavernous front room — which looked, in the glare of the fluorescent lights that night, too wide and lofty and tiled a space to ever be adequately heated, or even thinly warmed. This prediction proved accurate. When the temperature there was ours to control, we discovered that it didn't matter if we placed both our on-loan space heaters in the room and cranked them high enough to singe the links of the feeble electrical system: We would never manage to take the edge off that chill. But in the end, the cold didn't really matter. If anything, it came to seem a necessary, albeit uncomfortable, aspect of the apartment's obstinate charm. Life there would be as raw as that at the summit of a wind-blasted cliff, I imagined then, and again was more or less right in my estimation.

After glancing at the rest of the apartment to be sure that our first charged impression had been correct — we agreed that we would take it. There were two large rooms, a hallway of a kitchen, and a basic bathroom with a ragged piece of broken mirror propped on the primitive sink. The place had some furniture (a boxy Formica-topped desk, a stuffed couch, several rigid chairs, and a drafting table from whose weak back we would soon learn to eat our meals, taking extra care not to set pots down suddenly and upset its nervous balance), but still it echoed, hollow as an airplane hangar. Even after we scattered the floors with the candy-striped rag rugs we'd toted back under our arms from the Old City, the front room talked back when we whispered. A child's desk and rickety trundle bed took up most of the back room, whose most magical feature was a wood-and-glass-fronted cabinet, set back into an arch. When we visited that first night, its papered shelves served as a resting place for what looked like most of E.'s belongings: a few rolled floor plans, a sweater tangled in its own tattered sleeves, some notebooks, several pairs of worn tube socks. A plastic-framed poster of a David Hockney swimming pool leaned against one wall, its electric new blues and yellows at once worlds away from this turn-of-the-last-century Arab house and, in a blockier, more abstract sense, a perfect extension of the building's deepest shapes.

E. seemed reluctant to make the place his. As we sat and discussed the lease and security deposit, we sipped the tea he served us from what appeared to be his only two cups. He coiled his arms around his legs meanwhile and squeezed himself into a tight knot on the couch, unwilling, it looked, even to let his feet touch the floor. I had never owned property, but I thought I understood E.'s impulse to flee town just as soon as the apartment was officially his. It wasn't that he didn't love the place; as he showed us the views from the bedroom windows and the faint scar on the floor where he'd knocked down an extraneous wall, it was clear that he did. He just needed to leave and come back, I supposed, to prove that this was home.

We ourselves had, in a way, set out on a similar probative trek. By packing all our books, plates, lamps, rugs, and paintings into a San Francisco storage locker and flying with the key to Jerusalem for ten months, we were testing the bonds and limits of our American home. Peter had a fellowship to translate medieval Hebrew poetry from Muslim Spain. His stipend would pay our expenses that first married year in the city where he had spent the better part of his adult life and where I'd lived briefly as a student. He would finish his book; I looked forward to improving my Hebrew and, just as important, to not being in San Francisco, where I had moved, fresh and confident, straight out of college, and found myself almost instantly at loose ends.

While I couldn't blame my newfound confusion on anyone but myself, I sensed there was something in the slack rhythms,

the soft air, and famous fog of that city that encouraged aim-
lessness. Was it something in the water? Almost everyone I
knew there was caught — if that's not too active a word to
describe this floaty way of drifting through life — between
careers or lovers or coasts. Nothing stuck. Or perhaps I should
say, nothing stuck to me. There were others, obviously, who
were quite content to pass the time there, and though I took an
active dislike to the local cult of the good life and its literary
equivalent, I tried for a while to adapt myself by searching out
and soaking up the more grounded sides of the city: I'd stroll
past the herbalists, fish stores, and stationery shops of
Chinatown or buy my fruit, cheap and in Spanish, from the
outdoor stands in the Mission District. There was an Iranian
grocer named Muhammad from whom I often purchased salted
white cheese, pickled vegetables, and powdery cardamom
cookies. ("Your husband is Persian?" he asked skeptically once,
as I loaded my goods on the counter.) But these (mainly commercial) wanderings of mine had a haphazard quality. The
neighborhoods were not my own, and my own wasn't quite
mine either: We lived, at the time, in a liminal area that Peter
called the Tendernob, at the peculiar, anonymous midpoint
between the seamy, druggy Tenderloin and upscale, patrician
Nob Hill.

My occupation also seemed, for the first time in my life,
fuzzy, even pointless. When I'd first arrived in California, I
worked at a magazine where I wrote rejection letters by the
stack and learned to proofread — both inherently depressing
tasks, as they make one fixate on all that is *wrong* with a given
paragraph or poem. Later, I assembled indexes, edited text-
books, taught Hebrew school, and worked for a while as a
receptionist in an imposing Victorian mansion where illegal
immigrants would come for help in getting their green cards.
Surrounded by the heavy, plush drapes and mahogany panel-

ing, I sat at a huge desk and answered the phone, then tried to decide, on the basis of a few nervous words mumbled in one of twelve or fifteen languages I didn't understand, where to transfer the call. To the Cantonese-speaking social worker or the Mandarin one? Vietnamese? Thai? Polish? Serbo-Croatian? When the phone wasn't ringing I would read. Once, in the midst of a biography of the poet Mandelstam, I looked up to find a gaunt young man inspecting me and my book scornfully from the bench where he slumped, waiting to talk to Ella, the sweet, pudgy Russian counselor whose bright pink lipstick only emphasized her full mouth of gold teeth. Finally, he spoke: "You are not Russian." No, I said. "You have interest in this poet?" Yes. "But you do not know Russian language." No — which prompted an exasperated shake of the head and a lengthy lecture, in broken English, on the superiority to all others of his native tongue. This literary-jingoistic diatribe — from a person who had, in fact, come to wait opposite me in the hope that he might someday win American citizenship — veered now to the subject of Shakespeare and culminated in the conversation-killing pronouncement, "Is much better in Russian." Who was I to disagree? My internal sense of continental drift had become so pronounced by then, I could hardly defend Shakespeare's language, let alone my own.

Throughout all this, no matter what my paying work, I spent several hours a day forcing myself to sit still in a claustrophobic little lean-to I'd rented, attempting to grind out my fictions. Few of these efforts took: My subject matter felt random, my narrative gaze blurred. (Was the Novel dead, or was it me? I honestly had to wonder.) Chekhov, I'd heard, had once written a story a day for one hundred days. I too would write a story a day, and I did so, for a few weeks, that is, till my ideas dried up, and I began to sense the words evaporating even as I scribbled. At one point, as if to rub in my own sudden loss of nerve and focus, I taught a correspondence course in expository writing to precocious seventh- and eighth-graders. I never once laid eyes upon my students, yet their strong personalities asserted themselves through the loopy, pinched, or jagged script that covered and spilled from their envelopes, and through their often hilariously self-assured prose, which, in a rather frightening way, reminded me of myself at a certain, cocky age. "My first novel was a derivative affair, a minor historical trifle," one thirteen-year-old aspiring romance writer explained for me in her swirly purple hand. "But my second is, I feel, a much more mature attempt. Might I interest you in a copy?" As jobs went, it was entertaining, though the epistolary nature of my relationship with these kids only added to my out-of-body sense of myself in San Francisco. For all they knew or cared, I might as well live in a Nebraska log cabin. This pleasant, mild, defiantly nonchalant city was getting to me, I announced to Peter. (As soon as I said it, I felt relieved, as if I'd been running a low-grade fever for months on end and had only noticed it now.) Perhaps we should leave for a year. He agreed readily, relieved in his own way, as he'd made it clear to me and to others that while the streets he walked were San Francisco's, the map he followed in his mind still belonged to Jerusalem.

And while we told ourselves — and told E. that evening, as we wrapped our cold hands around the hot cups and contemplated the ceilings' impressive height — that we would return to California come summertime, the words sounded tinny and a little far fetched when uttered inside that cavelike Middle Eastern room. San Francisco seemed farther from me now than almost anyplace on earth, whereas (for reasons I could not fathom then, and only begin to understand now, much later) after just a few minutes, this place — that is, E.'s faded couch, with its ill-fitting blanket for a cover and several tattered throw pillows — was already oddly familiar.

⟩⊗⊗⊗⟨

The floors of the apartment were covered with an almost invisible layer of dust that had landed when E. razed that extra wall and, despite my various attempts to sweep it and scrub it away, the particles remained, pale and stubborn, until the end of our stay there. The dust was just one of the house's defiant elements — the cold was another — signs that we mere renters would never conquer the oldness and vastness and slightly archaic grandeur of the building, which seemed to have been constructed with obedient servants in mind. I felt weak, short, and mutely humble as I struggled with the broom.

But I felt tall and absurdly omniscient when I stared from our windows. There were seven, all told, six of which had rounded tops and long, graceful sides, sunken into the walls like the colored openings in the sides of a church; one was square and no bigger than a fishing boat's porthole. The windows possessed ghostly, calming properties: Standing still and looking out, I had a peculiar feeling of privilege at being able to peer at the world from above, as though I truly had come to rest at the earth's epicenter, the Jerusalem of the medieval maps. This was, I like to think, not snobbery but the flush of refreshed perspective, since what I could see from my perch was not really a view, in the obvious tourist-snapshot sense of the word, but an average landscape made breathtaking by my enchanted angle. True, the apartment did sometimes offer a few more predictably stunning landscapes. On a clear day it was possible to drag a chair close to the second window in the front room, stand delicately on it, pitch to the left, and catch a corner of the chocolate-wrapper gold that glittered from the Dome of the Rock. And one needed no chair at all to see how the trim, obelisk-shaped tower of the German-built Augusta Victoria hospital cast down a haughty colonial sneer at the spilling Middle Eastern city below.

One of the bedroom windows faced directly out onto the noblest, gentlest, airiest, most softly shushing eucalyptus tree that I have ever known. Sometimes a few menacing crows would circle her branches, cawing and smacking their wings as if preparing to rumble. But when they took refuge on opposite sides of the tree's abundantly delicate leafage, they grew quiet and suddenly mild, chastened almost, by the huge poise of the eucalyptus, the way she whispered and dipped, shivered and laughed in the breeze.

The other bedroom window watched over a sturdy, gingerbread-styled church whose roof was rimmed with ornate curls of ironwork and dainty carved scallops. Three perpendiculars poked out from the baked tiles, providing a kind of raised tripartite agora where the pigeons perched in clusters: a skinny metal TV antenna, a chunky cross, and a short bell tower capped by a rusting weather vane. It was a compact building, a solid, rectangular box whose stones exuded a steady lemon light, set back from the street on a neatly tended patch of greenery and flagstone, and partially hidden on our side by a crumbling old wall and a cluster of weedy trees of heaven, which looked to me — with their awkward trunks and bursts of pointed leaves — pubescent, like date palms in training. We rarely saw people coming or going from the church but, on Saturday afternoons, when most of our neighbors had retreated indoors for their post-big-meal nap, an ecstatic chorus of vigorous voices would pour through our windows for hours on end, accompanied by an amateur accordion and a thump-thumping upright piano. They were Finnish evangelicals who sounded tipsy, like grinning revelers on a merry-go-round; theirs was a fine, full, simple song in the most major key imaginable, as far north as the ear could possibly travel from the haunted, mounting, elemental drone of the half-dozen or so muezzin calls that would wail from nearby East Jerusalem, overlapping, intersecting, piercing our sleep just before dawn each morning, then buzz four more times to the tops of our heads every day.

But mostly what I saw when I peered out our windows were other people's rooftops: the rust-red sea of tiles leaned against tiles, with water heaters propped like giant tin cans on enormous slanted shelves. There were occasional dainty white splats of pigeon droppings from above ("as if an angel had been sick," Peter quoted Mina Loy for me, and her words made special sense in that somehow celestial apartment), and the mossy filigree that rain and strong sun will bring with the years. All the houses had similar arched metal shutters that swung shut to close during the hottest or wettest parts of a day, though it seemed that each family had selected, as a kind of crest or coat of arms, a different shade of blue or green or cherry paint with which to cover their tin window flaps and the wrought-iron, curlicued gratings that nestled inside every opening.

Most astounding of all was the sky. Could it be the same mild stretch of space that hung above the streets down below? Living beside it meant subjecting one's moods to its whims. Roiling gray storm clouds would mass, then yield to dainty flecks of cumulus; pungently chilled air heralded rain, in its season, and during summer the hot desert wind would creep through our windows, making movement a strain.

Once, though, we were foolish enough to leave the house in the midst of an especially brutal late-May *hamsin:* We stumbled, sun-blind, down the empty streets, then, realizing our mistake, tripped back home, our arms thick with the heat, the small paper bag of Arab honey cake I'd bought from a peddler just inside the Jaffa Gate now a gooey, leaking mass in my weary fist. After closing the shutters one by one, gently, so as not to aggravate the distinct tom-tom sensation that boomed at our temples, we lowered ourselves onto the bed and closed our eyes. Eventually, as we lay there, the house's antique cool began to enter our bones, and we thanked those impervious walls as we drifted off to sleep.

>⊗⊗⊗<

We soon met our neighbors on the top floor. In fact, every time we opened the front door we met our neighbors. The upper balconies and catwalks ran into each other in a way that made constant chatty interaction an unavoidable part of every day, although after a week or so of bidding a curt *Good morning* and *How are you, it looks like rain,* I began to notice that the other women who puttered on their porches with laundry, trash bags, and wilted floor rags never started conversations from distanced beginnings, the way Americans do. Neither did they adopt the intricate swirls of formal blessing and greeting with which the old men would regale each other as they shuffled back from synagogue early each morning. The women simply picked up a sentence where they'd left it off the day before, in the no-nonsense tones of family members too familiar with each other's sorrows to pretend to such canned niceties. Although I recognized the difference between my manner and theirs, I never managed, or really wanted, to change the way I spoke to them: My Hebrew was still halting, and I understood that attempting to mimic their molten familiarity would be much more insulting than the crime of seeming a bit cool and foreign. It would be presumptuous to think I could gab as loosely as women who had known each other for at least the length of my entire life.

Nehama, whose name means "comfort," lived next door with one of her grown sons and her husband, who rarely made an appearance on the porch, but who would nod to me and smile archly when I saw him wandering through various neighborhoods downtown, his elegant bald head topped by a tilted cap, his posture loping but strong as a teenage boy's. What was he doing, I wondered, biding his time in these different city parks? Was there something to avoid back at home? His bearing was at once aristocratic and relaxed, in an Old World way that's unique in Jerusalem to the aging North African men with their canes, their hats, and their *sheshbesh* boards, and to the frail little Central European ladies, who will smooth their coif and pin a brooch to the lapel of their best blazer before they set forth from their cramped apartment for an afternoon stroll to the corner, and back again. The philosopher's "purposeful purposelessness" describes well their carefully choreographed perambulations.

Nehama was a jolly-seeming young grandmother with dark auburn hair, a burst of freckles across her nose, and a sweetly husky voice. Of all the neighbors, she was the friendliest; she had an easy, gentle bearing and seemed to understand my discomfort with the language. A nursery school teacher, she was probably used to baby talk still a good deal more basic than mine, and she spoke clearly as she tended her plants, a row of geraniums she was coaxing to bloom near the railings, without much success.

Often after my early-morning Hebrew class I would meander home through the *shuk,* both in search of the fresh makings for lunch and to clear my head, stretch my limbs, focus my gaze after hours of numbing desk-sitting. Then, arms heavy with fruit-and-fish-filled plastic bags, I'd make my way back to the Daniel Street house, up the stairs, past Nehama's dry-looking flowerpots, and into our apartment. One day, well into our stay — it was a springtime afternoon and warm enough to keep the front door open, as all the neighbors did in this season — I threw my things down and progressed to the kitchen, where Peter and I began to clean the kilo of blue-green sardines I'd just bought. The BBC World Service bleated from the radio in the front room and we talked as we eased the guts from this small school of fish, filling the sink with micalike piles of transparent scales and briny-smelling entrails. When we were through, I washed and dried my hands and left the kitchen to hunt for my pocketbook, which I came to understand was no longer in the house. Someone — who? — had slipped inside our open door and spirited it away.

A few hours later, after scouring the house from top to bottom in futile search for the missing purse, and after listening wearily to Peter's agitated assertions that he'd *told* me not to leave my valuables so close to the front door, how could I be so careless, I stepped out onto the narrow balcony and found, just inside the white metal gate, a plastic bag with my purse tucked primly, almost apologetically, inside. The conscientious thief had relieved my wallet of its bills then taken pains to return the rest — the credit cards, American driver's license, roller-ball pens, and tube of Chapstick. The addition of the plastic bag added a strangely personable, almost gallant, flourish to the crime. What kind of thief, after venturing through an open front door and exiting with a pocketbook, feels enough shame to try to hide his crime inside a plastic bag? Why return the purse at all?

But it wasn't really such a difficult case to crack. I guessed (and Rina, another neighbor, confirmed, with a set of the most overwrought pantomimed gestures I'd ever seen, a spontaneous torrent of grimaces, wagging fingers, and headshakes) that Nehama's son — an army-aged young man whom I knew only by the dark back of his head and the loud Pink Floyd he played early in the morning and late at night — had taken and emptied my pocketbook. To this day, I can't be sure if it was him or his embarrassed mother who tucked the bag inside the plastic sack, like a school snack, and slipped it inside our gate, but I think I know.

Several years later, after we'd decided to stay on in the neighborhood and had loaded the contents of that San Francisco storage locker onto a ship that sailed due west from Oakland to Ashdod, we agreed — driven more by curiosity than by any sudden desire to prove ourselves good citizens — to attend a meeting at the local community center. Held around a long, low table dotted with plastic plates of sesame-covered pretzels and sandwich cookies colored a queasy yellow to represent vanilla, it was a noisy, drawn-out affair that veered from boisterous laughter to fierce accusations to bureaucratic yammering and back again to laughter.

To an outsider, the meeting might have looked ordinary, like any other conducted weekly in dozens of school and synagogue basements throughout the city, around the world. Then again (on second glance, even the stranger would see this), the neighborhood itself was far from ordinary, and the messy history of the place informed the very heated pitch and pace of that day's discussion. Musrara was built under Ottoman rule at the start of the century, mainly by well-to-do Muslims, though with time it also became home to Christians, Armenians, Greeks, and a smattering of Jews, who all lived there together in relative luxury and harmony throughout the years of the British Mandate. (The place was, I'd read, fashionable for government officials in the twenties and thirties.) Then the neighborhood was split down the middle by the war in 1948. After the original residents fled or were driven out, depending on which historians one chooses to read, the eastern side became a part of Jordan, while the western was hastily appropriated as stopgap — soon to be permanent — housing by the Israeli government, which settled large, homeless families of Jewish immigrants from North Africa in the structures that had remained standing when the fighting stopped. Mostly Moroccan, poor, and traditional in their religious practice, these new arrivals had been shipped into the neighborhood straight from transit camps, where the conditions were squalid and where they had been doused with both literal and symbolic DDT. As a general rule, the European establishment considered the new arrivals from Morocco at best primitive, at worst diseased — in either case, clearly in need of socialist-style reeducation and lessons in hygiene. Their Easternness, as well as their religious predilections and penchant for superstition, it was believed, posed a direct threat to the well-irrigated Western utopia that Ben-Gurion and his secular comrades were busy sowing in the desert. And it wasn't just the authorities who patronized the newcomers. Other immigrants looked down on the Moroccans as well — the bookish, Mozart-loving areligious Germans, the middle- and upper-class Iraqi merchants, even the impoverished refugees from Hitler's Eastern Europe, who had simply never encountered Jews so dark in their appearance and so Arab in their manner.

But looks were deceptive, and the Moroccan Jews themselves were, on the whole, determined to distinguish themselves from "the Arabs" — an extremely general term, spanning as it does a complicated range of nations, religions, and classes — whose language and culture they shared and alongside whom, by their own accounts and with few exceptions, they had lived quite peacefully in the old country. Here, though, things were different, and a pecking order was quickly established. *You don't know them like we know them* was a fairly standard racist line, offered up in the face of various attempts to promote friendly coexistence between Arabs and Jews. *Thieves! Liars! They just want to throw us into the sea.*

Such prejudice was especially distinct in Musrara, with the Jordanian border just one street over, sniper fire frequent, and eight or ten people often forced to live in a single room. Granted, "the Arabs" were hardly to blame for this intense congestion, but the grievances of the locals ran together and boiled in the rash, vague way that such desperate complaints often do. Whether their sorry lot was the fault of European-born Labor government functionaries or the fault of "the Arabs" was a mere technicality: *Someone* was to blame.

Poverty and proximity to no-man's-land, though, did not prompt a single, blanket response. At the same time that many residents of this rough border zone grew to be unabashed (even proud) bigots, the neighborhood was also home to some of the most outspoken critics of exactly this sort of chauvinism, Eastern Jews who saw in the suffering of the Palestinian people a connection to their own plight. The Israeli Black Panthers came from Musrara, and they made the neighborhood famous as a place of fervid social unrest, an area that many Ashkenazi Israelis, rightly or wrongly, considered physically dangerous. This stigma was so pronounced that, decades after the barbed wire had disappeared, the angry demonstrations ceased, and the neighborhood begun slowly to integrate, I got into a taxi and told the driver to take me to Musrara, and he refused at first, insisting that I must have the address wrong. There was no reason that I — that "a girl like you" — should want to go to Musrara. But I live there, I told him. "No, it can't be . . ." he argued for a while then finally admitted that he himself had grown up there. When his parents died, he and his brothers sold their apartment and he bought a big house out in the suburbs. But he cursed the day he left Musrara. "I was an idiot," he said. "To give up such a house, such a neighborhood. There's nowhere else like it."

Although the east of the city came under Israeli control in 1967 and the border migrated to a more distant remove, the streets of Jewish Musrara had only just now been repaved, the sewage lines fixed, a few small parks planted, and the residents granted economic incentives to fix their decaying stone houses or refurbish the insides of their cramped apartments in the low-income concrete housing "blocks" that were built at the center of the neighborhood in the midfifties to help ease the crowding. The renovation process constituted at once a face-lift and open-heart surgery of sorts, as the residents turned from destitute charity cases to middle-class homeowners in the course of just a few years. Meanwhile others, like the taxi driver, saw this gradual process of gentrification as their ticket out, and sold their apartments, leaving the neighborhood for roomier, newer, more ostentatiously bourgeois climes. As early as 1948, the government had even concocted a new, symbolic name for the neighborhood, to replace the old, literal one, so fraught with troubling associations — but nobody ever called Musrara (which means "pebble-covered" in Arabic) by this loftier, made-up term, Morasha (which means "legacy" in Hebrew). Nobody, that is, save a few real estate agents and the organizers of this meeting — who in daily conversation referred without hesitation to their home as Musrara but now called proudly to order the latest assembly of the Neighborhood Committee of the Morasha Community Center. This PTA-styled gathering seemed a stiff and somehow alien way of officially addressing problems that, not so long ago, had been the cause of angry demonstrations and riots in the streets — once or twice even brutal, crippling assaults on city officials by locals with home-made weapons. We were the only rookie residents, and the only Ashkenazis, seated at the table, but the old-timers seemed intent on conducting business, for their own benefit, in this formal, newfangled manner.

After reports on the day-care center, the tutoring programs, garbage pickup, and half a dozen other items on the agenda, Nehama, who'd sat gossiping with her friends throughout the gathering, suddenly raised her hand to speak.

She started to talk in the softly upbeat way she had, nodding and smiling to her right and left, as she suggested that perhaps the group should consider establishing a committee to assist the families of drug addicts, who were, unfortunately, statistically, still so abundant in our neighborhood. She knew people, good, responsible people whose very own children were addicted to all kinds of poisons. Maybe a counselor or a social worker could offer assistance, could give some kind of advice . . . And almost before she managed to eke out her official proposal, her voice cracked and split down the middle and she began to sputter, then sob with a series of short, jagged gasps as she let loose the story of her own son, the *narcoman* ("junkie" in Hebrew, from *narcotic;* the term always conjures a vulture-swarm of etymologically unrelated but tonally linked death words in my head: *necropolis, necromancer, necrophilia*). His wife and children were left hungry and alone while their father wasted away. And her other son — my probable purse-thief — was wrestling with a similar problem. She didn't know if it was better or worse that he had no wife and children to harm with his habit, to steal from and starve and abuse . . . But the families, the *families,* she wept, are miserable, their pain, their hurt . . . As she continued, her friends tried to calm her. She shivered and shook but never once sobbed the saddest word, *I* . . .

Perhaps Nehama's agony startled me because she'd politely kept it locked inside until the outburst at this meeting. Afterward, too, when I passed her near the newspaper kiosk or as she chose chili peppers at the local vegetable stand, she'd smile, tip her head to the side, and look cheerful, asking warmly how we both were and leaving me to wonder if I'd dreamed her quivering public breakdown. Our other neighbors were hardly so restrained. Rina, for example, would let her troubles rip in loud belts and shouts across the balcony, blasting the whole building with her complaints as she cranked up her favorite cassette of screechy Turkish music, yelped by a twelve-year-old pop star who went, like a stripper, by just one exotic first name: Yala or Zaluq or some such.

Rina was fleshy and nearsighted, with dyed scarlet hair pulled into a bushy ponytail on top of her head, and the huge, commanding voice of the madame at a Baghdad bordello. Unlike most of our neighbors, including her own husband, she was Iraqi, and she made sure, with the help of her megaphonic vocal chords, that everyone for several blocks knew it. She wore flowing robes of printed cotton, red polish on her fingers and toes, and usually teetered across her balcony in a pair of cork-heeled platform shoes, with thongs capped by two paste-on silver daisies. She kept her door open at all times, a state of affairs that bothered me at first — when she yelled at her husband or sang along with the radio, the sound of it echoed against the back wall of our apartment — but for which I was profoundly grateful the day I was cooking alone in our house and sliced open my thumb with a sharp kitchen knife.

Without thinking twice, I ran out of our apartment, through the gate, across the walkway, and onto Rina's balcony. Her radio was blasting, and I clattered inside the open door as I'd seen her little grandchildren do on numerous occasions. "Hurts! Finger!" I wailed, reduced in Hebrew to age three or so, as I held the seeping digit before me.

Neither Rina's distracted expression nor her gruff tone of voice registered even the slightest hint of surprise at my sudden inarticulate appearance on her doorstep, and for once I was so comforted by her nosy, bossy demeanor I could have wept my gratitude: In my wounded state, it felt fine to be barked at to Sit down! Drink this! (She slammed a tall glass of impossibly sweet lemon soda before me and I gulped it with my good hand as if it were mother's milk.) She then marched the length of her immaculate kitchen and, from one of the many drawers that lined the marble counter, produced a wad of cotton and a tin of ground black coffee. Here! She thrust me the fluffy ball, dipped in the pungent particles, and I obediently applied the weird balm to my wound. Almost instantly, the bleeding and my tear-ful hiccups slowed. She filled my glass a second time and ordered me to Drink!

When I was calm enough to speak, I apologized and thanked Rina through my giggled half-tears, admitting I'd acted like a baby, maybe the cut wasn't really so bad. Pah, she continued to putter, arranging a stack of powdered-sugar cookies on a plate she then set before me and insisted that I sample. What are you saying? Her *Mah pitom?* meant, literally, "What, suddenly?" — an expression that implied not just the English *don't mention it* or *not at all* but suggested, too, the ruffle of offense about to be taken, as a cat's back curls in warning: as if by denying the depth of my cut I was in some sense demeaning her hospitality, or hinting that there was any other way she could have reacted besides immediately, unquestioningly, with lavish generosity, when her usually aloof American neighbor appeared, sobbing and slashed, at her front step. I tried and failed to imagine the same scenario repeated, blood and all, in the San Francisco apart-ment house where we'd lived for almost three years and barely nodded at our neighbors when we passed them in the hall.

I sat with Rina for an hour or so, and she gossiped to me, if not exactly with me, the whole time, commanding me now and then to try another cookie or drink some more mint tea. She seemed a different person inside her own kitchen — a bit softer, less territorial, more girlish. And she clearly liked me better when she could nurse me and bandage me and fill me with refined sugar. I liked her better that way too, although in the weeks following, as the skin grew back across the gash on my thumb, I felt a ticklish flush of embarrassment every time I saw her. I smiled politely and murmured hello, but could never bring myself to come sit at her kitchen table again.

><><

The final apartment on the top floor belonged to a fat, smiling woman who rarely ventured beyond the balcony, but who was tended by her grown daughter, Dvora. The daughter was also large and shared her mother's slightly mongoloid features, as well as her stringy hair, cut in straight bangs across her fore-head like an oversized rag doll's. But as we soon learned, Dvora's slow, lumbering looks were deceptive. From behind her thick plastic glasses, she saw, knew, and perhaps understood more than anyone in the building.

In the beginning, she frightened me in ways that weren't fair or rational, but that I couldn't help: She seemed possessed — whether by demon spirits or merely deep thoughts, I didn't know — but her lugubrious bearing unnerved me, and my heart would pound melodramatically whenever her apartment door creaked open. She shuffled everywhere in house slippers with tight-fitting nylon socks, barely blinked, and spoke in a guttural whisper. Twice a week, on shopping days, she'd emerge from the apartment, lugging a shopping cart behind her, dressed in a voluminous flowered housedress, her lips smeared with bright red lipstick in what seemed a single grotesque concession to sprucing herself up for the outside world. Maybe she had designs on a neighborhood guy and had painted her mouth for him. Seeing her decked out so, my fear began to fade and embarrass me, and I hoped for her sake that, if a crush were indeed the unfortunate case, she wouldn't bump into its object today, with that gunk smudged so helplessly across her lips.

It took her several months to acknowledge our presence in the house, but when she did, it seemed that we had passed some rigorous private trust-test of hers. How-are-you? She would fix me squarely in her gaze and direct the words right into the cores of my eyeballs. I was fine, I'd insist, without conviction. And how was she today? At which she would look away, bless God's name, and trudge off. That was all we ever said, until a knock came on the door one day. When I answered she was standing there, a bit to the side, her eyes fixed at me. In her inching whisper, she asked if we ("you and the Mister") would be home later today. She had something she needed to ask of us. Of course, I said, but wouldn't she rather just come in right now?

"I-will-be-back-in-one-hour," she intoned, lurching off in aching slow motion, her chin tucked low into her chest.

And after exactly an hour had passed, the same flat knock came at the door, followed by the same sharp look when I opened. Dvora stood with her market cart behind her, its contents covered by a thick blanket. She checked over her shoulder several times before entering, then darted, with the lithest movement I'd ever seen her execute, yanking the cart over the high threshold behind her. "Goodafternoon," she whispered, her words suddenly pressed tight together. "I have a very important favor to ask. But you cannot tell a soul —"

When, some four minutes later, she'd checked the front entrance a few cautious times and tiptoed heavily from our apartment, we found ourselves in stupefied silence and sole possession of the entirety of Dvora's valuables — electrical appliances, jewelry, and mementos, I imagine, although, for all my curiosity, I never dared peek beneath their woolly cover to check what seemed to me this near-stranger's flattering but rather reckless trust in us. She and her mother had decided to make a rare excursion out of town for the weekend, and she — doubting the dependability of both the other neighbors and the sturdy-looking new security door she'd recently installed — had painstakingly gathered together every article of worth in her apartment, loaded up the cart, and wheeled it to us: us, the people she knew least well in the entire house — ciphers to her, careless tourists, CIA spies, or escaped criminals, for all she knew. It was ours for the weekend. She left a phone number where she could be reached "if anything should happen," and for the next few days her cart sat untouched in our back room. To exit, we'd walk crooked circles around it, as if it might be cursed or nuclear. We did not trust ourselves nearly so well as Dvora trusted us.

Whatever was or wasn't inside that cart, it was a relief when she came back and hauled it all off. She seemed a good deal more relaxed, too, after she'd recovered her mysterious belongings. She even invited me into her apartment, and I followed shyly behind, a little ashamed that I'd been scared of this good, harmless person before: She seemed childlike and sweetly excited as she led me inside. I wondered if, as a little girl, she'd had much occasion to bring friends home to play. Or had Dvora ever been a little girl? There was something unnaturally old about her, as if she had always been like this, wide and spinsterish.

Her house was quite literally spotless, with bleached white tile floors, a starched tablecloth smoothed at midweek across the heavy, Sabbath-meal table, clean-dusted chandeliers in each corridor, and several long runners of lollipop-green plastic ivy laced across the walls and up to the ceiling. She was bursting-proud of the place, that was plain: She took me into each room and stood, filling the doorway as she explained about the refurbished plumbing in the shower, the curtains she had sewn for her bedroom, the new refrigerator. I quickly used up my Hebrew words of praise and resorted to ahhing and mmming mechanically in vague appreciation of the apartment and everything in it. Then she led me, beaming, into the living room, where her mother sat ensconced on a fake-leather couch before the TV set, smiling at me and Dvora both, then turning back to her program with the same glassy grin fixed across her face. Dvora, meanwhile, had switched back into her throaty stage whisper and begun to extol her father, now dead, who was a hero, "very famous in this neighborhood" — I could ask anyone and they would tell me so. That was all she said about him, but in a torrent of associative pride-taking, she lumbered across the room to a shiny, lacquered cabinet with a glass front, and pulled from inside it a file of newspaper articles about our neighborhood and how it had changed in the last few years. Each piece had been clipped, folded neatly, and added chronologically to the file, which Dvora held gingerly toward me now in her big soft hands like some fine china piece.

"Once, people were scared to walk down our street. They were afraid of the drugs and the criminals. But now —" She gave me one of her piercing looks. "Now people from all over the world, from France and from *Am-er-i-ca* —" she squinted at me, "they want to come live here." She sniffed a little haughtily. "*We* have been here the whole time. *We* had no choice but to live here. *We* know this place. *Other* people come and buy houses and let their children play in the street, but *they* will never know."

With this defiantly cryptic speech, something in Dvora's slightly desperate bearing fell away and she stood up straighter, more imperiously than before. I wasn't scared of her now, but her words made me feel a bit skittish and light-headed, mothlike and liable to waft off in the next gust of wind or lofty declaration. Dvora suddenly looked bored by my presence in her living room (she had opened the folder and was painstakingly straightening the papers inside), so I pulled my gaze to the side and mumbled, "Thank you," finding my Hebrew had sputtered out. "For — everything." She smiled in her canny way, and watched me as I turned, fluttered across the walkway and back through our gate, over the threshold and into the dusty enormity of the apartment we borrowed that year.

A GOOD PART OF TOWN

when she learned we were moving to our very own apartment, less than a thirty-second walk from the house on Daniel Street, Dvora nodded gravely and said she'd heard that was "a good part of town." And once again she was right: Our new street, near as it was to the first, felt distant as another city in a faraway time zone. Living there, closer to the ground, we were subject to other winds, wafts of different cooking smells, the clockwork rotation and noisy overlap of separate sounds in the morning. It was a busier, soberer, even angrier place than the first. In the earliest gray light of day, a taciturn team of Arab city workers would roll garbage bins down the pitched flagstone street, which would later fill with the loud calls and kisses that followed the three children downstairs as they clattered off to school, banging the iron gate behind them with a gleeful crash. Then came the drone of the drill at a nearby construction site and the vague mutter of a neighbor's radio. Filtered through the thick walls, the announcer's words were garbled beyond comprehension, yet his agitated inflections survived the divider intact.

Inside, the rooms were warmer, the sky farther off. Even the dappled kestrels that housed below the drainpipes near our balcony seemed more aware of our proximity than their exhibitionistic cousins who had mated at eye level in the eaves opposite our old apartment. Every hour or so they had gone at it, with a sudden violent surge of flapping, beating, squawking falcon lust. The shyer birds at our new address, meanwhile, consented to nest in the attic catty-corner but would drift upward, toward the highest TV antennae, to procreate in peace.

Before it was ours, Shimshon and Tzipi had lived in the small apartment with their two solemn little girls, who each wore gold gypsy hoops in their ears and hand-me-down dresses that didn't hang right. Shimshon was a wiry boy of a father with bulging eyes, permanent stubble on his chin, and a desperate, rushed way of making a point. Born in this neighborhood, one of the youngest of at least a dozen children, he would stand too close when we met him in the street, and push his fingers into Peter's sleeve as he grinned nervously at me, gulping the air, loudly asking how I was, then rushing on with his sentence before I could answer. We sensed, and heard snatches of rumor to confirm the hunch, that he'd had trouble with the law and that the black satin skullcap he now planted like a beanie on his close-cut head was a new, though frantically heartfelt, addition. In the neighborhood's previous tumbledown incarnation he had been a squatter in the apartment, had renovated it in haste with his own clumsy hands, and was sunk and sinking farther into debt. It was clear he needed money badly: Some thuggish threat to his physical safety seemed likely, and although he muffled his panic most of the time with a battery of darting, jokey gestures — his elbows slashing space whenever he spoke, his sneakered foot jiggling as soon as he sat down — his bearing would turn somber, almost funereal, whenever he huddled on a street corner, absorbing the mumbled admonishments of one of his older, bearded brothers. The neighborhood was full of them, these menacing middle-aged men with narrow hips, protruding bellies, accusing stares, and Shimshon's family name. As we worked to develop a tentative, businesslike relationship with Shimshon, the oldest of his siblings had already stepped in and informed Peter hotly of his contempt for all *Ashkenazis-like-you*. Another brother was, I was almost certain, the mastermind behind the blunt sign posted near the yeshiva where he supposedly studied (in actuality, he spent most of his time smoking cheap cigarettes, drinking black coffee, and muttering conspiratorially with the other rumpled students, none of whom appeared terribly interested in mulling over the finer points of Rabbi X's understanding of the God-given need for crop rotation), NO PARKING: UNAUTHORIZED CARS WILL BE DAMAGED. I never heard the particular stern, scolding words that they poured into Shimshon's ear on these whispered occasions, though his expression, as he listened, would dull and go blank with a look of numb fear.

A few hours later, he would make a "casual" appearance near our Daniel Street apartment, ambling as nonchalantly as he was able. Did we know the plumbing in the apartment was less than a year old? The new balcony would add ___ square meters to the land registry size. He was ready to sign whenever we were. Would we be ready soon, did we think? Today? Tomorrow? We wouldn't want to miss out, there were other people interested, didn't we understand? *Very interested . . .*

Shimshon couldn't fathom, I'm sure, the dizzy terror we felt at the thought of buying these rooms, of signing on the dotted line and calling them our own. And secretly, a little guiltily, I was grateful for the plain old-fashioned sexism that typified our interactions and precluded Shimshon's doing business with a young, childless woman like me, as long as I had a man around to do the talking. So the nitty-gritty of the negotiations and cash transfers fell to Peter, as did the jittery, almost daily stand-offs with Shimshon, who would raise his voice, grow suddenly red, and erupt into bellows at the slightest, generally most base-less hint of danger. Western and modern as the apartment-buying process had seemed at first, with its maze of certified agents, notarized contracts, appointments with the lawyer, and prices listed in dollars, the exchange of money and property was, it became apparent, just a paper-pushing version of the oldest, most primitive of ancient tribal bartering rituals. Not only were the women exempt from the rite, the men circled each other suspiciously, prepared, if their wounded honor demanded, to resort to the sword. I had never seen my usually gentle husband so close to a fistfight as he was after several of these encounters, just as I had never imagined myself adopting the stereotypical, sticky-sweet role of the worried little wife, nervously cooing at her agitated mate while she attempts to loosen the defiant knots that his hands have become. We were, I see now, both tem-porarily crazed.

Deep down Peter might have felt the same jumpy fear as Shimshon, but he was also wise enough to keep his glowering moods to himself, or between us. In the other man's presence, meanwhile, he hid his frayed nerves behind a skillfully placed mask of cool authority, a clever facade he'd almost mastered while teaching English to rambunctious Israeli high school stu-dents. After one especially nervous and hostile day, which the two began together on the mortgage bank line and ended by walking home in silence on opposite sides of the street, like some vaudeville duo at a loss for new gags, Shimshon came scrambling back to the other sidewalk and pleaded to make up. Ultimately, I think, it was Shimshon's childish need to be liked, no matter how humiliating the consequences, that kept Peter from ever just punching him in the jaw: It was hard to stay angry for long in the face of such reckless vulnerability. As soon as the official business was complete, the papers signed, and the apartment legally ours, Shimshon, visibly astonished by Peter's ability to converse in reasonable tones with our lawyer, a soft-spoken Virginian Jew with Groucho Marx eyebrows and an unflappably gracious manner, declared that my husband had missed his calling. He, too, should have been a lawyer. Meanwhile, Shimshon's wife, Tzipi — decked out in her best dress and heels for the Friday-morning closing — seemed confused by the law school diploma that hung on our attorney's wall: "Are you also a *doctor?*" she asked.

Tzipi was pregnant again and, despite Shimshon's hysterical displays, she remained as smoothly unruffled by the whole extended legal transaction as a plump hen, warming her eggs. A dark, pretty woman, with young skin and an old figure, she liked to wear vivid lipstick and confine her cheerful conversations to two well-worn topics — childbearing and body weight — both of which relied, in her eyes, on the express will of God. This house was lucky, she told me: *It brings children, Adina.* (She attached my name to the end of almost every sentence, a habit I imagined she must have developed from delivering round-the-clock orders to Shimshon, or, as she called him *Shimshon-did-you-hear-me?*) Here she was, ready to give birth to her third little one, thank the Lord, in this heat, oh, it was tough, eh Adina? . . . not that she was complaining. We should be so lucky, with God's help, the apartment was good for children, Adina. Did I think she looked fat? Every time she started to lose weight, she'd find out she was pregnant, thanks to God. *What can you do, Adina?* Thank the Lord. It will work out. Shimshon's a good father, this is a good house, her children are good children. In the end, everything, *ev-er-y-thing*'s good, thank the Lord. Was I hungry? I should eat. I looked skinny to her. . . .

We were not sure at first that we wanted the apartment. The air hung in a peculiar static way, especially in the midsummer heat. Shimshon had imposed a strange airlessness on the place when he renovated. He'd tried his hardest to make the elegant old rooms feel new, in the temporarily shiny style of cheap children's toys, as if a set of flimsy cabinets and cut-rate bathroom tiles would triple the worth of the simple, cavernous spaces, designed to be left wide open and cool. Every day Tzipi sponged the floor and stripped the beds but, no matter her possessive pride, the family still seemed like squatters in the apartment, ready, if need be, to pack a few things in a satchel and flee, leaving no fingerprints. A huge television set dominated the main room, flanked by two large, empty pink decorative urns and a white plastic lawn table with chairs to match. There were amulets everywhere: the inverted hand of a good-luck *chamsah* here; a framed poster of the wizened Moroccan holy man, the Baba Sali, there; simple *mezuzot* in every door; and by the entrance, an inky kabbalistic charm in childish, sloped letters listing eight names for God, plus *ha-shem ha-mifurash*, "the Name Pronounced," which is to say, not really pronounced but summed up in cautious shorthand. Even after we moved in and knocked down Shimshon's makeshift walls, added a thick butcher block to the kitchen, four-meter ceiling-to-floor bookshelves in Peter's study, a painted ladder up to the storage loft that would serve as my own miniature office, and, in the entryway, a delicate old set of wooden double doors with colored-glass panels, we kept Shimshon and Tzipi's charms exactly where they'd left them — too superstitious and quietly grateful to fiddle with the fates, about which Shimshon had warned us just before he relinquished the keys, pulling Peter aside to whisper loudly that the doorpost blessings should not, under any circumstances, be toyed with, altered, or removed. He was telling us, he sternly announced, for our own good and for the *peace of the house*. It was an odd way to phrase a wish for our well-being, as if the inert stone and plaster required divine protection more than we ourselves. Nonetheless we listened and heeded. When Shimshon left the apartment for the last time, he behaved the same way he always did as he passed across the threshold, though this most ordinary religious gesture struck me for once as almost unbearably poignant, perhaps the calmest and least-tormented act I'd ever seen the overgrown delinquent perform: He touched his fingertips to the doorpost scroll then softly brushed them to his lips and kissed the house good-bye.

Tribal and familial rhetoric gave the place its sentimental shape, but to live comfortably there, day to day, demanded a willed building of invisible walls. The endless, clamorous neighborly contact that might have seemed quaint or colorful in the course of our first honeymoon year spent as tourists on Daniel Street took on a vastly different — and far more maddening — form once we'd chosen to stay put, find jobs, pay our municipal taxes. One had, at a certain point, to imagine oneself alone in one's little sphere or risk a constant sense of violation, the invasion of the precious "space" that Americans covet but tend not to appreciate fully until it is missing.

There were various means of erecting walls. First, there was the literal way. I sewed curtains and Peter planted a border of strategically placed fruit trees — lemon, pomegranate, olive, kumquat — as well as a palm and several laurels in the huge tin, terra-cotta, and painted plastic pots that we'd collected around town (as discreetly as possible, sometimes at night, from a construction site nearby). Within one growing season the branches of these saplings provided enough leafy privacy so that we could sit, talking with friends, protected from the view if not the sound of our neighbors, who lounged just a few feet away, arguing amiably on their own balconies.

Then other, mental walls demanded construction. I learned, for example, to turn my gaze from the window when our closest new neighbor, Rafi, a chubby, bespectacled bachelor a year or two short of retirement from his civil service job, sat down in his striped pajamas to eat the simple meal his elderly mother prepared him every night just in time for the eight o'clock news. (She herself seemed never to eat, or at least not to eat at that table.) Chipmunk-cheeked Rafi had a gimp leg and one shriveled arm that he held before him as if he were permanently preparing to shake someone's hand; his mother was a shrunken woman with a slight hunchback, bow legs, and a clean cotton scarf that she always pulled low over her forehead like a picture-book pirate. They kept their balcony door open in the evenings and lived near enough so that I could read the time from their wall clock with its swinging pendulum that clanged erratically on the hour, once every couple of days. I could also distinguish the plaid pattern on the plastic tablecloth where Rafi ate his salad and see the triangular tin stand that the mother always kept stocked full of colored paper napkins.

For a while I looked on, newly fascinated each night, at their silent supper ritual. But with time I realized what every stage actor knows and reminds himself before he sneaks a peek at the audience from behind the drapery: *if you can see them, they can see you.* Hoping Rafi would also practice a bit of restraint when the opportunity arose to spy on us, I taught myself to look away.

I could not, though, completely squelch my urge to eavesdrop. While most of the time Rafi and his mother were safe from my nosy ears by simple dint of the thick and incomprehensible-to-me Moroccan they spoke with one another, an occasional conversation would sift through the air in emphatic Hebrew. Their use of the local language seemed related to Rafi's moods: When he was irritable he would insist on speaking

Hebrew, which he commanded and his mother did not. She would either counter with her own insistent Maghrebi dialect, or answer in basic, conciliatory Hebrew. So too there were practical household words — *plumber, antenna, refrigerator* — I recognized, and the usual religion-drenched blessings and greetings called out to friends who passed under the narrow balcony where she sometimes sat peering down, her chair pulled to the edge. One day, from inside the apartment, I heard the mother rhythmically incanting a shopping list — cabbage, parsley, dried apricots, Princess of the Nile fish — which Rafi then repeated, in the same pregnant tones, to be sure he hadn't missed a thing before he set off for the *shuk* with two empty canvas bags dangling from his good arm. On warm-weather Saturday mornings, after he left for synagogue, his mother would sit on the porch with a dog-eared book pressed close to her failing eyes and would talk plainly — it took me some time to realize — to God, as a child who has just learned the alphabet might read aloud to her doll. Occasionally, she'd erupt into song, and no matter how often I overheard this ritual, the sound was always startling — a gusty, full-throated melody that suggested possession by benevolent spirits and seemed to bear no relation whatsoever to the faint little voicings we'd barely hear the dainty matron mouth during the rest of the week. Later, after her other grown children and small grandchildren had come, blessed the Sabbath wine, eaten loudly, and gone, she would scrape the plates in silence and Rafi would nap noisily, filling our large porch with the stereophonic grunt and whoosh of his wheezy snoring.

While I was content to sit in selfish quiet and snoop on the sounds from the apartment nearby, Peter and Rafi had developed a more friendly and upright relationship — ignoring one other when the occasion demanded and then, at designated times of the week, suddenly greeting each other across the bougainvillea bush with formal yet genuine enthusiasm. (On Friday evening and Shabbat the whole neighborhood turned into a more loosely sociable place, and the salutations called across balconies were at once freer and more elaborate.) Rafi approved of our sprawling porch-garden, despite its aggravating effect on his allergies, and he took care to commend Peter on its development almost every time they spoke. Perhaps, he suggested once, we would like to run a wire across the alleyway and let our jasmine grow toward his own balcony? It was actually a rather shocking proposition, given the extreme tidiness of his porch and the slightly unkempt state of our own: By lacing the flowers across the divide, however narrow, this natural boundary between us might be erased, and petals, to say nothing of dirt, would be sure to fall on his mother's immaculate tiles. Sensing that maybe he'd ventured a step too far with this rash horticultural proposal, Rafi never mentioned the hanging gardens again. Instead, he would stand at polite attention, gripping the newspaper in his good hand, and ask about our health, or explain with a sheepish sort of pride about the high school equivalency exams for which he, just months from his pension, was studying. In the last few years, he had arranged through a special workplace program to take and pass the matriculation exams in English and math, and now he was trying to master the history curriculum. This was proving more difficult. He had failed the test once before and spent the last year patiently retracing his steps through the textbook. It was hard to absorb all those names and dates. But worthwhile, yes, definitely worthwhile: *better late than never,* he declared in the prefab proverbial style that accounted for so much of the courteous Hebrew spoken in our neighborhood. Rafi formed his sentences more carefully than someone born into the language, and he meant the truisms he uttered, animating them with his gently forceful delivery and dignified posture.

Living this close to another family, I began to feel much the way I had with the kestrels on Daniel Street — both embarrassed and fascinated at being able to watch so much intimate behavior so closely. Our neighbors were, needless to say, far more complicated creatures than the nesting birds, and our radical physical proximity was deceptive. The more I learned about the eating habits and communicative quirks of Rafi and his mother (whose name, that most basic of neighborly intimacies, it occurs to me now I do not even know), the less, I realized, I understood about them. That is, as Rafi's napping, TV watching, and bickering schedule became second nature to me — providing a sort of constant, busy backdrop to the patterns of my own daily cooking, cleaning, talking, reading — the more mysterious the two seemed, even with the few tangible facts from Peter's conversations with Rafi thrown into the speculative stew. And the unabashed audibility of the mother's prayers only compounded my sense of humble wonder at being able to see so much while I fathomed nothing at all.

When one of our other neighbors told me of Rafi's father's suicide, he did so in the respectfully ominous whisper used by the locals for talk of untimely death, no matter how many years after the fact. As he said it — in a rush, using terms that seemed intentionally evasive and short on detail, as if specificity about such mortal matters only served the deadly winks and blinks of the evil eye — I had the uneasy sense that I'd actually known all along. No one had told me, till now, and there was absolutely no hint in the humdrum putterings of the odd couple across the way to suggest tragedy — although, of course, the minute that thought crossed my mind I canceled it out, annoyed with myself for the naïveté, even stupidity, of assuming such long-lived sufferings would announce themselves physically in the here-and-now as they did in a horror movie or gothic novel, with low moans filtering from the rafters in the night or invisible door hinges creaking. If anything, Rafi and his mother lived in a home that seemed, at least from the outside peering in, well lit, cheerful, and unusually sweet-scented, with the smell of soapy floors on Wednesday giving over to the cinnamon and honey wafts of Thursday's baking, and the rich, meaty stew-cooking savor of Friday and into Shabbat.

Had these domestic rhythms always been so upbeat, or were Rafi and his mother attempting to fend off gloom by acting especially happy and relaxed, aware at some just-conscious level of the curious, nearby presence of my own and other spying eyes? Did Rafi's father also exude an air of routine contentment, even as he plotted his early demise? And had Rafi sat since childhood in this particular dinnertime chair, or had his father's death demanded that he take over the patriarch's post and position, in all senses, eating the same salad at the same time each night, facing the same green refrigerator and reading the same newspaper, maybe even exchanging a few of the same abrupt words with the same woman, loving wife, doting mother? I was ashamed of these questions: I couldn't know, could only imagine, though I also couldn't help asking. Later, when Rafi's mother tripped in the street, banged her head, and slipped into a coma from which she never recovered, I was overcome by a flood of mute empathy as I watched our neighbor puttering in his pajamas through the silent rooms. He spent his days at the hospital, by her bedside, and when he came home at night he looked exhausted. He opened the door to his balcony less often now, and when he did I could barely allow myself a furtive peek. It was different, sadder, more twisted somehow, to spy on a man when he was alone. Out of a blend of guilt and concern, I wished at first to offer him some friendly token. A cake? A box of bourekas tied with white string? These perishable gestures seemed paltry next to his impending orphanhood. But then of course it dawned on me that Rafi must know we were there, across the street. Now I saw that he opened his door for the express purpose of *not* feeling so alone. To glance now and then in his direction was, in fact, the neighborly thing to do.

Besides, Rafi was not unique in his sudden solitude: Our street had known many more than its share of freakish or abrupt deaths. Not a supernaturalist by nature, even I had to wonder if the place was haunted. Our neighbors themselves seemed a bit spooked, though again not by white-robed ghosts who popped up and shouted "boo" but by something — a memory perhaps, a phantom ache, or a constant, gut-level longing — that etched the faces of those around us with subtly wistful lines.

Downstairs from Rafi lived Nomi, for instance, a glum-looking jeweler who would drag from her green studio door to her nearby car with distracted movements, her graying bob pitched low to the ground, shoulders rigid. Sometimes she would smile tightly when she passed me in the street, and sometimes appear not to notice me at all. Although she was one of the other "Europeans" in the neighborhood, we spoke to her only occasionally and always in low, steady tones, without elaborate greetings, about dry matters like garbage pickup or tree pruning. She seemed "nice" in the indistinct way one thinks of decent-seeming people one doesn't know well yet doesn't feel inclined to warm up to, and her son was easily the quietest, most elusive kid in the whole neighborhood. I rarely glimpsed the boy, and knew little about him except that for a brief while he was learning to play the recorder. The painfully tentative scales of his practicing filtered into our house around dinnertime, after which there came nothing save a blank silence from Nomi's. And when, after a few months, the child abandoned the instrument completely, we heard no sound from down there at all.

Nomi's husband had also killed himself — which was terrible on its own terms but especially eerie when recounted in one breath with the tale of Rafi's father upstairs. Having taken place so close to the other, self-induced death, his suicide did not seem to belong to the realm of psychology, and suggested circumstances much stranger, almost beyond his control. After I'd heard about what had transpired on both floors next door I understood better Shimshon's insistence that we not touch the *mezuzot,* for the peace of the house. Perhaps the walls *did* have a say.

But these spirits did not, again, outwardly spook the street so much as lend a sad, hushed edge to the boisterous noise and bustle everywhere. Even the four rowdy children upstairs had this private spectral reserve. The two prematurely faded teenage girls and the two little boys they raised in the absence of their mother (killed in a terrorist carjacking the year we moved into the house) and father (a tall, shifty man with too-blue eyes, a young girlfriend, and a bellowing voice that he'd desperately turn on his children whenever he made an occasional appearance at home) were haunted. Not that one could see this from just looking at the extranormal guises they carefully cultivated. The girls wore bright halter tops and platform shoes and would sing along loudly with the radio or laugh on the phone with their friends; the older boy was lithe and suntanned, a junior-high-aged soccer fiend with a charmlike necklace of sharpened teeth (of a dog? a shark?) always fixed at his throat. These three seemed visited by a nurturing force — the absent presence of their mother, perhaps, who in life, by all accounts, had been a woman of unusual goodness and poise. The damage only announced itself at nighttime, when the shouting and crying fits began, or when one encountered the littlest boy, Matan, as he wandered the neighborhood, wreaking havoc in a businesslike manner, or shooting imaginary Arabs with his plastic gun. A pale child with dark bangs and very red lips, he was too young to remember his mother, and although his sisters and various aunts and grandparents would turn up periodically to ply him with Popsicles, muss his hair, or call him inside for dinner, he seemed well on his way, at age five or so, to serious trouble. His seemingly sweet disposition could shift abruptly and without change of expression to an off-the-cuff, matter-of-fact form of kiddie sadism: He tortured alley cats, threw rocks at the birds, and pulled down his pants in the middle of the street, peeing a flamboyant arc in the direction of a group of shrieking girls as they scattered. Once or twice I called out his name to stop him in the middle of one of these awful routines — MATAN! WHAT ARE YOU DOING TO THAT PIGEON? — at which he would hesitate, look up in a vague haze at the horrified stranger's face before him, then silently amble along. Attention might have been what he craved, but he seemed altogether unimpressed at having gotten it. I had, if anything, spoiled his fun, broken his concentration. These worried scoldings left me feeling especially helpless and busybodyish, and after a while I stopped even trying.

And then there were the shades who left no trace all, in some ways the scariest. After the suicide of the teenage boy who lived alone just across the street, an air of muffled panic hung in the air, and even before the week of mourning had passed, the terse, pasted notices announcing his death (BLESSED IS THE TRUE JUDGE . . .) had vanished from the stone walls, as if the slightest trace of peeling paper might prolong the curse that obviously plagued the family and, by extension, our block. Every mention of his name and death must be physically scraped off and washed away.

Later we learned — not from our suddenly reticent neighbors but from a sensational all-names-have-been-changed-to-protect-the-innocent-styled story in the weekend newspaper — the long, horrible tale of his sexual abuse, suicide attempts, and, finally, "success," planned to coincide with the anniversary of the hanging death of an older brother. I felt sorry then, and also, in a not completely admirable way, relieved that I could not for the life of me conjure the image of the miserable boy whom I had surely passed dozens of times in the street but whose face I could no longer see.

THE MAYOR
XXXXXXXXXXXXXXXXXXXXX

most of our neighbors took time to warm
to us. But no one made us feel more welcome than Meir, the
local grocer. Almost right off — from the first morning I stumbled out to buy bread, butter, and a box of long-life milk — he
insisted we make ourselves at home here, in his home, a place
generously defined not just as his own
store but the whole closely knit neighborhood, the entire ingrown country. An
effusive set of hellos and salutes greeted
each customer who passed into his shop
— in physical if not psychological fact
just two narrow aisles crammed with
merchandise. It became clear upon entering the store, though, that Meir's honor,
his family's honor, and maybe even the
honor of his long-dead ancestors was at
stake with each and every bubble-gum
sale, and soon we, like almost everyone
in Musrara, had become friends of a

commercial but genuine sort with the shopkeeper and Yaffa, his
eerily intuitive wife.

Meir had grown up in Musrara. Then, not so many years
ago, as a newlywed, he'd opened his "mini-market" and emblazoned in crimson letters across its yellow awning YAFFA, much,

perhaps, in the way a boatman christens a new vessel with the name of his lady love as a final good-luck touch before setting out to sea. Meir's Mini-Market Yaffa was, in my own admittedly biased estimation, the best grocery store in the entire city: not just because Meir and his lanky Arab assistant (whose name and face changed every six months or so but whose height remained the same, as if Meir hired with tall shelves and hard-to-reach canned goods in mind, no experience necessary) made sure to stock the dairy refrigerator and bread bins freshly every single day, but also because Meir was such a pleasure to buy yogurt and tinfoil, chickpeas and vinegar from. Cookies and pastries arrived warm every morning from a bakery nearby; farm eggs, some with a few wispy feathers still stuck to their shells, sat stacked in their open cardboard flats; the high tin shelves were always dusted and filled with boxes, sacks, jars, and tubs of the simplest and most essential stuff; even the Hebrew tabloids looked edible there, laid out in their crisp, inky piles. The only really frivolous items in the shop were the brightly wrapped chocolate bars and packets of hard candies, the bottles of lollipops and licorice whips, arrayed in tight rows across the sliding tops of two huge blue Popsicle freezers. Although one sensed from this lavishly sweet display Meir's soft spot for his own small children and by extension all the children in the neighborhood, these confections too were a serious matter. A good part of Meir's business, during the summertime in particular, came from the under-ten set, who seemed to survive for the season on a diet of nothing but sunshine, sugar, and colored ice.

While other stores in town might have boasted more exotic and varied merchandise, none I'd encountered was quite so neatly or proudly organized. There was little wasted space, all the goods at Meir's meant to be bought, consumed, and replenished right off, though my frequent visits to the store did prompt in me the urge to squirrel away items I knew I didn't need. I often found myself contemplating packages — of coconut flakes, dried figs, sesame crackers, red lentils, bulgur — for which I had no obvious use but which looked so appealing in relation to the rest of the store's unpretentious inventory that I had to restrain myself from buying them for their own sake, in the name of abstract plenty. The sudden urge to stockpile that struck me upon entering the store was not, I see now, a matter of greed or gluttony, but followed from Meir's own bearing. It was impossible to conceive of a growling stomach while sheltered inside Meir's retail pleasure dome, yet just beneath the offhand surface of each of his cottage-cheese transactions lay an awareness of the acute necessity of every item sold and bought. It was with a sense of quiet gratitude, not luxury or indulgence, that one placed one's groceries on Meir's counter and waited for a tally.

And if Meir's shop wasn't satisfying enough on its own terms, one needed only to compare it with the other "mini-market" nearby — two streets down and worlds away — to understand its literal and symbolic superiority. This second shop was more typical of the city's grocery stores, a poorly stocked little box of a place run by a well-meaning but sluggish man named Mani and his rather sour wife, who always slumped on a stool behind the counter with the unfocused sneer of someone who has been startled awake before getting a decent night's sleep. Mani seemed resigned to his role as the neighborhood's lesser grocer, and he invested most of his limited energies in rearranging the counters and freezers once every couple of weeks. While the floor plan kept changing, the food itself sat for too long on the shelves, going stale if not bad and giving the whole shop the grimly desperate air of a survivalist's pantry — an impression underscored by the building's close proximity to a municipal bomb shelter. Located at the bottom of the same incline that

Meir's market crowned, this other store owed its continued existence solely to topography. The local stragglers, those who couldn't be bothered to venture the slight uphill grade to Meir's, shopped there for their staples: presliced white bread, cigarettes, cola. Sometimes on mornings when I didn't feel like giving my mind over immediately to upbeat conversation and just needed some milk for the coffee already brewing on the stove, I too would trip the path of least resistance and find myself skulking into Mani's, plagued most times by a pang of melodramatic guilt. Patronizing this sad-sack spot was, I knew, a betrayal, not just of Meir but of all that he stood for — pride, care, determination, even art.

So most days I found reason to buy something from Meir the master grocer, both for the sake of that something itself and my own social well-being. And if ever I found myself short a few coins, or even bills, Meir would sternly insist I take what I need and pay him back later: "Are you *sure* you don't want something else? Some juice?" (He knew well my repertoire of usual purchases.) "Do you need some cheese? Don't be embarrassed. Take, take." Mayor, we renamed him privately, the mayor of our small city-village, for his easy yet politic charisma and unflagging ability to make anyone who passed under the circus-tent-like awning flaps and into his shop feel fortunate. This even-handed welcome, or canny business sense, even extended to the realm of national politics and the pictures that he chose to display above the cash register, alongside a slick ad for Swiss-style yogurt, a popular kabbalistic bumper sticker, and his neatly handwritten Hebrew exhortation to have a GOOD MORNING, GOOD AFTERNOON, GOOD EVENING, GOOD NIGHT, THANK YOU VERY MUCH AND GOOD-BYE. After the last elections, he had dutifully tacked a shiny paper portrait of the new right-wing prime minister alongside the fading portrait of the old left-wing prime minister, for whom he himself had voted. "So no one should talk," he explained when I remarked at the unusual sight of the two sworn enemies smiling side by side. Later, though, as the political situation worsened and each party leader fell from Meir's favor, he removed both their faces from his shop wall, and replaced them with a safer long-term bet, a large framed photograph of a white-bearded Moroccan rabbi in an elegant conical hat. *"Khalas,"* said Meir this time when I asked, the terse Arabic for "enough," with which I had to agree.

Still, in general he avoided sticky political or religious discussion and preferred to keep the talk in his store focused on more upbeat matters. He managed the shop and the conversations that took place there as if this were a party and he were the host, responsible for keeping the mood light and music flowing. Sometimes he would shush a tirade about to begin and steer the truculent speaker back to a friendlier subject: the weather, the lotto or soccer results. When he discovered I worked as a film critic, he had a convenient new topic to trot out in a conversational bind: movie stars. *What do you say about the new Schwarzenegger? Sharon Stone, do you like Sharon Stone? Al Pacino! Now* there's *an actor . . .* Rude neighborhood children, confused American tourists, sunburnt Romanian workers, stooped Arab grandfathers, bleary-eyed civil servants from nearby City Hall, me — he treated us all to the same casually measured banter that he directed at his cronies, a ragtag group of layabouts whom he had grown up with and, it seemed, considered as close and unshakable as his own brothers. In various tipsy formations, this lazy crew would gather around the sandwich counter at his store most evenings to stand, drinking whiskey and wolfing down the little black olives and peeled cucumber slices he set out on a saucer and replenished as customers shuffled in for a few last items before closing time. Sometimes he even served his buddies entire hot dinners that he would spontaneously conjure from one or two ingredients lifted off the store's shelves. The men had usually grown quite rowdy by this time and would drunkenly croon some synagogue song as they pushed the stacks of newspapers and piles of soup mix and cookie packets aside, pulled up chairs around the table that served as an extra counter, and awaited Meir's latest pungent concoction: white rice and tomatoey-sweet beans (from a can, yet transformed in this magical context into a great delicacy) or perfect circles of parsley-green *ejjah,* thick Moroccan omelettes cooked on the small orange camp stove perched on a stool just behind the counter. Mint tea followed, poured into glasses from a dented but sparkling tin pot with an elegantly curved handle, after which — I do not know. Perhaps this straggly men's club picked up and carried on elsewhere, when the other customers left and Meir locked his shop doors, although by this hour he himself usually seemed anxious to close up and get home to his wife and three little boys whom he plainly adored more than anything on earth.

With his baby-fat padding and full black mustache, Meir still looked young, but he already carried himself as a kind of tribal-elder-in-the-making, a breed apart from his drinking buddies who grew louder and sillier as each of these evenings wore on and the whiskey bottle's contents lessened. Meir, too, would sip the harsh local liquor from a little glass near closing time and allow it to mellow his mood. But as he counted the money in the till, stowed away the outdoor cake and newspaper racks, placed a final telephone order for the next day's rolls and bread, and bolted the front doors behind him, he stayed more or less sober. One had the sense, in fact, watching him in constant thoughtful action that, no matter how much of the cheap booze he gulped down in the name of friendship, he had lost the ability to ever get really drunk. He had too many details pressing on his mind. Although his demeanor was always outgoing — either jolly or agitated, but never turned inward — the better I knew him, the more I understood that running the little grocery as cheerfully as he did was a tremendous, grueling task, made all the more daunting by the sleight-of-hand that allowed him to appear most often in high spirits. Meir loved his work, that was clear, but that love didn't shorten his fourteen-hour work-days, or make it any simpler to demand credit payments from some of the neighborhood's shiftier residents. For the first few years that we shopped at his store no one, so far as I could tell, was denied a running tab by Meir, who kept track of what was owed and paid in a neat black box beside the register, but whose fundamental sense of the need to prevent his neighbors from going without food was occasionally tested by an espe-cially snaky shirker, or by the most unapologetic bill dodgers, who would send their smallest children to collect the items on a list as a last-ditch means of further stalling payment. Meir couldn't very well refuse a six-year-old her request for tea bags, frozen peas, and laundry soap. The child, often too young to read, would hand Meir her mother's list like a bank robber's stickup note and wait, understandably a bit confused by the whole transaction and her own role as an innocent go-between. More than once I'd heard him bellowing into the phone at an "old friend" who pleaded sudden insolvency and appealed without shame to Meir's already-overextended sympathies. (And what about the friend's sympathies? Meir had a business to run.) Another time I listened as he explained with weary firmness that the customer on the other end of the line could *not* pay off her grocery bill with used stereo equipment. Soon after, a terse sign in Meir's own hand appeared, announcing NO CREDIT GIVEN HERE, once and for all. The declaration didn't seem cold so much as necessary, a weary step that Meir had in essence been forced to take by people more cavalier about their debts — both financial and emotional — than he. He'd tried his hardest to help his friends and neighbors and too many of them had let him down, and though I myself had only rarely and always skittishly bought on credit, making sure to pay up within twenty-four hours, I too felt responsible, as if I were partly to blame for the collective abuse of his overwhelming goodwill.

Not that he ever complained to me or to Peter. The closest he came might be a mumbled confession of slight fatigue, or a general *What can you do?* murmured late in a slow day of a particularly hot midsummer week. One just knew, though, that his job was endless and arduous: Even when he was struck with a second heart attack, Meir insisted on returning to work after a scant and, I gathered, extremely restless week in bed. *How are things, Adina? How is Peter? What's new? Send my best, a warm hello* — he welcomed me, upon his own return, before I had time to greet him. Meir's well-being might have been threatened directly by the wear and tear of these grueling days, but he refused to buckle, insisting (implicitly, by his constant charismatic presence) he was well enough to stand upright behind the counter and greet his customers by name as they trickled in throughout the day. Any rest cure a cautious doctor might prescribe was emotionally useless.

Yaffa, his wife, also had a regal bearing. She was naturally shyer than her husband, or at least more obvious in her introspection, a trait unusual among the shrill young mothers of our neighborhood. There was, too, a cloud of just-perceptible sadness that sometimes shadowed her face, making it difficult to say for sure if she was depressed or simply daydreaming. Yaffa took her public role far too seriously to ever grumble or detail specific woes from behind the cash register, but she also couldn't prevent the trace of her bluer moods from seeping through the politely cheerful facade she'd learned from her husband, to whom boisterous sociability came as second nature. Late morning and into the afternoon, the quietest patch in the store's brisk day, she would relieve Meir of his post behind the counter, and when I sauntered in for a can of tuna fish or package of white cheese, I'd find her sitting very still, inhaling the silence and her cigarette as, in the summertime, the industrial-sized fan ruffled her dark ponytail and the papers on the counter. In the winter she worked all day in a long wool coat. Although she adopted a slightly formal tone with me — asking laconically how I was, then handing me an unnecessary receipt after ringing up my items and thanking me in careful Hebrew when I paid — I sensed in her presence a kind of bedrock understanding, despite our real differences. Her eyes would meet mine and she'd smile slightly as she placed my things carefully in a large plastic bag and wished me a good day. When she was pregnant, and in the weeks just after Meir's latest heart attack, she would sit in the same chair, pitched forward intently, reading psalms to herself in a barely audible whisper.

There was something good-witch-like about Yaffa. Her name — and by extension the mini-market's name — means "beautiful," which seemed unfair to me in the beginning, given how plain she looked at first glance. But the longer I knew her, the more the name seemed prophetic, a kind of slow-seeping secret to be revealed only later to those she trusted well enough to grace with one of her sudden, dazzling grins. Then her entire face would light up, her brown eyes glitter, and her whole being shine for an instant, radiant.

The first time she flashed me one of these smiles I was caught completely off guard, aware at some dim but happy level that the awkwardness of our limited relationship had lessened and that our connection had progressed, if not to real friendship then at least to real, unspoken affection. She had just given birth to her third son, and Meir — beaming ecstatically behind the counter late one afternoon when I wandered in to buy orange juice for a predinner screwdriver — invited me and Peter to the circumcision, to be held the next day at a banquet hall on the outskirts of town. I was moved, probably more moved than was altogether reasonable or appropriate. He had doubtless invited half the neighborhood, any familiar face that had happened into his store that day. At the time, though, this didn't matter. The simple fact that he considered us part of the neighborhood in this invitation-worthy way moved me. As he carefully copied down the address of the hall and the time of the festivities in Magic Marker and "with the help of God" I realized that, for better or worse, Peter and I had both already made other plans and wouldn't be able to attend. But I thanked Meir several times and took care, a few days later, to appear at the store bearing the gift of denim infant overalls wrapped in sparkly paper. Purchasing this token, too, had taxed me much more than it should have. I'd spent the better part of an afternoon wandering downtown in search of the right present, then paced the floor of the kids' clothing store unsure about the amount I should spend, the size of the baby, even the outfit's slightly precious French label: maybe it was too snobby, too imported-looking, too much. And perhaps it was an excessive gesture to give any gift at all. I understood well enough that my sense of scale was out of whack in relation to Meir and Yaffa. They didn't know it, of course, but sometimes my writing would keep me indoors all day and I wouldn't see another soul besides Peter until I emerged from the house in time for my dusk-hour run to their shop, ostensibly to buy soda water or a can of pickles but really to be sure to speak face-to-face with some other human being before the sky darkened completely. I felt so thankful toward them for simply *being* there on these occasions — calm, cheerful, and apparently unneurotic — that I guessed a gesture too grand was better than too meager.

And I guessed right. In thanks for my probably extravagant gift, Yaffa offered one of those full-wattage grins when she saw me next. Now she was full of familiar chatter and seemed more relaxed in my presence, greeting me each time I saw her with a soft burst of gossipy odds and ends, in themselves nothing special (one of the children had a rash, it was so hot today), but poignant in the context of Yaffa's typical reserve. Unlike the usual avid, undiscriminating local small-talkers, Yaffa's carriage was not automatically outgoing and jolly. It seemed as hard for her to muster this breezy nonchalance as it was for me to absorb it, and our mutual reticence linked us as a private joke would.

Although I'm sure Yaffa couldn't begin to guess how I spent my days, she seemed interested, which already set her apart from the other women in our neighborhood. I couldn't be certain but I had a strong sense that most of the rest of the nearby female population considered me at best inscrutable and at worst a sort of freak — possibly even the target of a curse — for not rushing to be a mother. Choice in such matters was more than out of the question: It was heresy. Barrenness would be better (biblical, even), and I assumed that most of them must have ascribed my "condition" to some incurable anatomical flaw, worthy of prayer and a few tongue clicks. Mazal, for instance, a blowsy Algerian neighbor who lived catty-corner and half a story above us and whose offspring numbered somewhere between ten and fifteen — I didn't try to keep track — offered a condescending smile one day as she watched me watering the porch garden and then called across her balcony in the most encouraging voice she could manage that "plants are *just* like children." Another neighbor-mother was distant toward me on the whole but allowed herself to greet me knowingly and ask how I was feeling when she once saw me balancing a liter of milk and family-sized tray of eggs on one arm: *Those* were quantities she recognized, and I'm sure she took the vision of me-with-milk-and-thirty-six-eggs as an announcement of my intentions.

And the unspoken curiosity about my childbearing potential was, we knew, conjoined in our neighbors' minds with whispered speculation about Peter's precise line of work. (I think they assumed I had none.) After watching my poet-husband intently tending our spilling jasmine, bougainvillea, and honeysuckle for several months, one man who lived next door and up one floor blurted his guess outright: "You work for the Society for the Protection of Nature!" No? "You're a florist . . . ?" Every time I passed our tubby yenta of a neighbor, Miri, in the street, she'd ask me nonchalantly how I was and was Peter abroad? She hadn't seen him in such a long time, after all, and she had begun to worry. . . . *Abroad,* too, had certain dubious connotations, vaguely financial. When yet another nearby neighbor was packed off to prison on a drug-smuggling charge (thus clarifying once and for all *his* precise line of work — which, based on the furtive hours he kept, the harsh fluency of the Arabic he used to shout at the construction workers forever drilling next door, and the unblinking deadness of his stare, I'd erroneously guessed involved the Shin Bet and violent interrogation), his little daughter developed an unnatural interest in Peter, roughly her father's age, to whom she announced that her daddy had gone to America. He did at long last return from those golden shores, looking tired and thin but bearing armfuls of gifts for his three blessedly oblivious children.

Yaffa, meanwhile, didn't seem to care about my maternal prospects or Peter's mystery profession. If anything, I sensed live interest in us as an unknown quantity — familiar foreigners or foreign familiars. Who, I wondered, did she imagine we were, this couple come from far away to settle down on her turf? The Russians and Ethiopians who spoke softly in their own languages as they padded cautiously down the slippery stone of the neighborhood's streets were part of larger, sociological trends and mass migrations that didn't require explanation. But why would secular-seeming Americans pick up and come here of their own free will? There were other Western transplants in the immediate vicinity, journalists mostly, reporters posted in Israel for stints of several years before their newspapers or TV stations shipped them off to some other continent. But they kept to themselves, spoke little Hebrew, and drove to the impersonal, multi-aisled supermarket to shop at all hours of the night. Most of them maintained a studied, even incurious, distance from the natives, whether in the name of reportorial objectivity or simpler contempt for the brash local manner, I was never sure.

It is possible, come to think of it, that Yaffa and the other seasoned residents simply didn't register the presence of this international secret society that passed stealthily through their midst like a band of haughty spies. I myself never saw its members in the street or at the bus stop; I knew of their existence only through my work writing film criticism for the local English-language paper, and from a few cocktail parties we had attended. There, though the tongue spoken was my own, the music, mixed drinks, and vegetable dip familiar, I felt more profoundly out of place than I did with our other, North African–born neighbors, from whom my differences were more obviously pronounced. One-on-one, some of the journalists were sympathetic, intelligent people — several of them were our friends — but as a group they frightened me: I didn't like the callous, know-it-all laughter that crowded the air when they came together and drank, the way the boozy generalities of their conversation sloshed from Jerusalem to Sarajevo, from Cairo to Moscow and back again (pat analysis of genocide and coups d'état overlapped with gossip about such-and-such a bureau chief whose wife had just left him). They boasted as they compared notes on famous people and places — each showing off his or her clever grasp of an entire culture in just a few parlor-game-length sentences. While I envied their confidence at some level, their glib attitude also angered me. With a smarting resentment that I'd try to quash with an extra plastic cup of vodka and too-sweet local tonic, I marveled at their collective ability to travel so far and so wide, and take in so very little.

How could they be so cocksure? We had lived for several years now on this narrow, cobbled alleyway, and I still barely felt I could account for the view out my own kitchen window, let alone the National Mood, the Prospects for Peace, or even the behavior of a couple of strangers as particular and vast in their complexity as Meir and Yaffa.

⚬⚬⚬⚬

The two of us rarely ventured into Meir's store together, yet once on our way home from a late-afternoon walk downtown we stopped in for a few dinner things, and Meir was for some reason overcome by the sight of us side by side — or, perhaps, of my husband in the flesh. Peter had been absorbed of late in his medieval translations and what he called their deep-sea-diving pressures, and had grown reluctant to run the gabby gauntlet that a trip to Meir's entailed, so I did most of the shopping. The longer my husband avoided the place, though, the more he dominated my conversations with Meir, as a kind of make-believe or mythical character, fodder for our casual talk, not unlike Arnold Schwarzenegger. *HowareyouandhowisPeter?* Meir would ask in one breath. Then he'd insist that I convey his best wishes to my invisible spouse. But now the recipient of these hand-me-down hellos was here in person and in honor of this rare event, Meir showered him with a far noisier greeting than the friendly but muted hello that my entrance typically warranted. After they shook hands and exchanged the usual *Hello, how are you, how do you feel, what's new, what's up, how's your health, and what's happening,* to which the answers were just as polite and programmatic — though genuinely warm — as the questions, Meir welcomed me by name: *Shalom, 'Adina,* the guttural *A* of the letter *ayin* gulped down correctly, as I myself cannot pronounce it. And then, without warning, Meir announced that "the time had come." We should, he declared, visit them sometime for a Shabbat meal.

I swallowed and left Peter to handle the appropriately imprecise acceptance of Meir's clearly stated yet somehow tentative invitation. We all felt a bit uncomfortable, I think, as soon as we'd completed this little ritual dance. The lines between business and friendship were always pleasantly blurred inside Meir's store, yet within a tiny, reliable range. One went on an errand to buy garbage bags or a loaf of bread understanding exactly what one ought to say and do. Now, the idea of transplanting this connection elsewhere, opening it out and confusing its familiar form, seemed reckless and even scary. It threatened our subsistence-level sense of ourselves in the neighborhood — the relaxed, unfussy shape of our daily interactions there, the chain of endless, unremarkable events from which we derived an enormous and essential sort of pleasure. What would we talk about over dinner? If it didn't go well, could I ever come back to Meir's and chat according to same old neat formulas? Though I felt close to Meir and Yaffa, in truth I'd never exchanged more than four contiguous sentences with either one of them or spent longer than five consecutive minutes in their presence.

There was also another, more primal aspect to our response — our dread, which we later admitted to each other as we made our way home past the ragtag, boys-only soccer game that seemed always to be in rowdy progress on the floodlit outdoor court that sat smack at the neighborhood's center. We lived, for the most part, on good terms with our Sephardic neighbors, though it was already plain to me that no matter how long we lived here and how much they liked us as individuals, we would always seem to them part of the same constitutionally withdrawn, allegedly well-off Ashkenazi elite. Or, at very best, we might be considered the exception to some basic, unflattering rule. Being Americans — initiates in the all-powerful free-market cult and also not, to their thinking, primarily Jewish — no doubt made us more acceptable. But what if, as guests of Meir and Yaffa, we revealed ourselves to be condescending snobs or panicked, prissy "whities" — not just in their eyes but, more devastating still, in our own? Aside from a spontaneous little Coca-Cola toast we'd drunk in the marble-tiled living room of our Moroccan-born contractor-neighbor, Yaakov, along with Ali, the neighborhood's dapper Palestinian fix-it man, over TV coverage of the signing of the Oslo peace accords, live from the White House Rose Garden (Rabin, Arafat, and Clinton each represented nationally by those gathered around this Jerusalem tube in a trilingual circus of simultaneous translation), none of our neighbors had ever formally invited us into their homes for a meal: to do so would mean venturing over some final ethnic frontier that both they and we tacitly understood was simpler left uncrossed. Yaakov's pillowy wife, who tended to bellow at her children in the same awesome, glass-rattling tones as her mother, Rina, our neighbor from the house on Daniel Street, grew silent when we entered, and offered a far-off smile, welcoming us with uncharacteristic formality before dutifully scrambling away to fill her best bowls with sunflower seeds and potato chips in honor of our arrival. She then wandered outside to smoke a cigarette and play with the baby, and made a point of not returning; her reluctance to sit and yack might have seemed haughty or cold to an innocent onlooker, though I'd already spent enough time in the neighborhood to recognize her standoffishness as fright — plain, blunt panic at the thought of interacting for longer than a few proscribed seconds with the childless Americans from upstairs, let alone with an Arab worker, no matter how charming or given to ironic winks Ali the handyman was.

There were neighborhood-business-related cups of coffee here and there, up and down the street, but they were few and far between (and by nature spur of the moment). But Meir's invitation was different. "The time has come" he'd said, which seemed to acknowledge in its drum-rolling though pragmatic way the very difference and difficulty I'm attempting to describe, the vault we were all poised to try to clear. In the meantime, though, his offer remained abstract and we half-contented ourselves with the knowledge that such spontaneous invitations were always being threatened in these parts and weren't necessarily acted upon. Mazal, the prolific matron next door, for instance, spent most summertime Saturday mornings swathed in a long robe on her balcony, brusquely insisting that various acquaintances who passed by come up and join her for tea. *Why not?* she'd demand to know if they declined, which happened most often. And no excuse was good enough: She pretended to refuse to believe they had another appointment, or an invitation elsewhere, and would use the gruffest terms to accuse the victims of her bullying hospitality of fibbing. It was part of a little game she played each week. *When will you come? Why not now? What's your problem? Come up here now!* And so she would begin again, with a touch of flirtatious anger.

But Meir, it turned out, meant it. (Later, I realized it could not have been otherwise: Meir *always* meant it.) Early in the next week, I finally overcame the fit of perverse misanthropy that had kept me from entering the store after his sudden demonstrative display and, as a sort of cosmic punishment for my antisocial behavior, I found myself alone with Meir, who I was sure had sensed my previous deliberate absence and now my creeping shame. First, he rang up my items and asked the usual polite questions about my health and my husband's. Then he softly suggested we come eat with them that Friday night. This time around, he sounded almost apologetic, though in a respectful way — as if to cushion the discomfort that he knew I must be feeling. As a man of his word he was, I understood, now obligated to host us. And I saw that we also had no choice but to accept. I did so, a dry smile pinned across my lips, then trudged home. Peter would be irritable about this development, I knew, annoyed at my bursting the private little work-and-newspaper-filled bubble of the weekend ahead. And in fact I'd had a perfectly legitimate excuse I'd forgotten to wield — a marathon of previews for an upcoming film festival, scheduled to run late into Friday night. But it was too late. As soon as I remembered my previous cinematic engagement, I knew I'd have to scrap it. The time, I supposed, had come.

✕✕✕✕

Although I would love to report that all our misgivings evaporated and gave miraculous way to pure public confidence in the days leading up to the dinner, the opposite is true. By the time the designated evening rolled around, we'd both worked ourselves into a quietly gloomy mood of anxious anticipation. After consulting with a friend better versed than we in the tricky soft-shoe of religious etiquette, we determined that a bottle of wine could be brought without offense. We each changed our clothes several times in nervous silence, then set out on the suddenly long-seeming journey several meters around the corner to the looming public housing projects where our hosts lived.

I had passed these monolithic gray buildings every day since we moved to Musrara, though I'd ventured inside just once in all these years. The place was, in essence, the sum symbolic total of all the impassable-seeming ethnic and class barriers that still existed everywhere around us. Though our neighborhood was in theory fully integrated, it was in practice still divided, as newcomers like us had paid handsomely to settle in the elegant old Arab houses with their scalloped lintels, interior arches, and high, sometimes vaulted, ceilings. Meanwhile, the two urban fortresses at the neighborhood's heart — boxy cement slabs constructed several decades before to provide the needy residents nothing more complicated than shelter — still belonged to the original occupants or their children and grandchildren, the only notable exception being a few slender-boned families of Ethiopians who'd moved in over the last decade. This was poor people's housing, and though renovations had recently been carried out on the buildings' facades — a decorative-stone false front stuck like a Band-Aid across the dirty concrete — there was no disguising the essential ugliness of the structures, or the basic character of the place as a home for those without the means to choose where they would rather live.

On most days, the long public balconies were filled with old women who sat in housedresses, head scarves, and spangled slippers, eyeing passersby from their stuffed armchair posts. Now, on Friday evening, this open-air living room was empty and we tiptoed past it, then up and down and around an interchangeable-looking series of empty hallways and institutional staircases several times before we found the correct apartment. Meir's instructions had been immaculate yet useless, since none of the building's entrances or floors were marked: We only found their home by asking an extremely pregnant young woman who ran through a list of possible Marcianos — Meir's brothers, cousins, uncles, apparently, who all lived within shouting range. She then gave our gift bottle of wine and my somehow foreign maroon dress a suspicious once-over and pointed us warily in the direction of the appropriate door.

The combined sounds of Friday-evening mealtime prayers, the nightly television news broadcast, the screech of a movie car chase, a few loud women's voices, and the wails of what seemed like dozens of crying children but might well have been just a noisy two or three surged up, jumbled, and recombined to form a dull yet omnipresent wall of noise. As we plodded upstairs, pausing at each landing to fumble in the dark for the timed light switch, it was impossible to say precisely where each of the parts of that racket came from. Meir and Yaffa lived on the top floor, and by the time we reached their door, the din in the stairwell gurgled all around our feet, a boil of human lava threatening to spill.

Inside, though, it was unnaturally quiet, as if the walls themselves were preoccupied with the thought of the delicate dynamic that was sure to characterize the long evening ahead, and Yaffa welcomed us with a serene smile that just barely masked her obviously threadbare nerves. The rich, layered scent of the food she'd probably spent all day preparing greeted us even before we knocked, and inside the apartment the smell was still warmer and sweeter. Meir had not yet returned home from synagogue, she explained in a slightly officious tone as she gestured us inside the apartment, whose central area was filled with bright oil paintings of flowers and familiar neighborhood landscapes. This space served the multiple functions of entryway, corridor, dining room, living room, TV room, and playroom for the children. Would we like a drink? Yaffa appeared at the sparkling glass coffee table with a large, new bottle of fine imported vodka — Peter's favorite brand, which Meir had understood we would appreciate. I felt a cheapskate's blush coming on at the thought of all the rot-gut alcohol I'd paid for with loose change at his store, along with cartons of juice to wash the stinging poison down. Meir, though, had selected in our honor a tall bottle of the very best, and priciest, stuff.

My anxiousness began to pass as Yaffa placed the bottle on the table and we were suddenly surrounded on the faux-leather sofa by her three peering boys, each neatly combed and scrubbed, dressed in a clean shirt and skullcap for the Friday-night meal. Ely, the eldest at age nine or so, was a small, stocky boss-man with probing eyes and a driven gait. He looked like a fairer version of his father and shared his carefully effusive demeanor. After steadily meeting my gaze, then Peter's, and introducing himself and his brothers in a comically formal manner, he sprang up to fetch glasses, then wrestled open the vodka cap and poured us glasses a little too full of the strong liquid. The uneasy air had already started to lift, and Yaffa herself looked amused and relieved at this precociously elegant bartending display by her oldest, but still little, son. She set out the requisite bowls of peanuts and potato chips then excused herself to attend to her chorus of burbling pots and pans. Meanwhile we sat on the couch between the boys, and Ely regaled us with a disquisition on his Sabbath routine: Most Friday nights he went to synagogue with his father, he explained, but tonight he had offered to stay and help his mother set the table. . . . He then disappeared into another room and emerged a minute later bearing his brother's first-grade penmanship notebook, which he proceeded to show off, ruled page by ruled page, with a bizarre adult pride at his younger sibling's scribbling crawl through the alphabet. "*Gimel,*" he said, "is already much clearer than *bet,* don't you think? Look at his *lamed!* Even better." Yonatan, the bashful author of the work in question, could only wrinkle his nose and throw a fistful of marbles across the floor in response. But Ely was unswayed and continued with the same patient, teacherly air — so peculiar for a child that I just nodded and reiterated his own words of praise, not in honor of his brother's fledgling hand as much as his own uncanny politesse. "And this is my favorite —" he announced with a philosophical hum. "A blank page. Unspoiled." His world-weary demeanor almost made me laugh out loud, but instead I forced my tongue against my teeth and took another sip.

And so Ely and his little brothers continued to entertain us until Meir finally appeared at the door in a larger version of the same pressed shirt and neat skullcap, booming with good wishes. The boys scampered off to jump on him like hungry puppy dogs and we rose stiffly from the sofa, each in our own way determined to make light of the situation's pronounced strain. (Amid the exuberant din of Sabbath greeting, Peter extended a hand to meet Meir's own and I smiled a little too widely.) The nonchalance we affected as we moved to gather around the dining room table and act relaxed in a respectful way while Meir blessed the wine and bread and his children in turn was, of course, transparently put-on: The awkwardness of our being there must have been as plain to Meir and Yaffa as it was to us. But so was our unspoken determination to push above and beyond this first level of strangeness. As we sat down, Meir, ever the diplomat, rushed to our rescue and perhaps his own with a torrent of insistently animated talk.

Meanwhile, with table-waiting help from somber little Ely, Yaffa served up the meal, which was — how else to put it? — quite simply one of the most satisfying I have ever eaten. It seemed endless, and describing the whole of it now — the array of cooked Eastern salads, the onion and egg pie, the tossed green salad, the peppery fish, the meat and rice and chicken and potatoes, the vegetables, the sliced fruit and hot mint tea — it sounds like a recipe for staggering gluttony, although in fact after each course, I'd consider myself completely sated, incapable of another bite, until Yaffa would appear, her expression at once eager and a bit concerned as she set down the next fleet of dishes before us. And then, again, I'd find myself ravenous for more, driven by a feeling of awe at the total, unstinting nature of the hospitality to which they had treated us, and an almost feverish sort of raw animal craving. (Whether or not I'd had my fill, I vowed to eat and eat.)

Throughout the meal, a place sat empty, waiting for Sa'adia, one of Meir's older brothers. I had heard, though I hadn't quite fathomed, that Sa'adia was a legend — not just in our neighborhood, but around the city and across the entire country. As a punkish teenager several lifetimes before, he had been one of the founders of the Israeli Black Panthers, a fact that at the time of our eventual meeting meant little to me, except in the most general and superficial terms. (Peter knew more, about which he remained tactfully silent.) Perhaps if I'd been less absorbed in my plate I would have intuited something of Sa'adia's stature, at least within the family, from the fanfare that preceded his entrance. Only later did I learn that Sa'adia Marciano, as ringleader of the Panthers, had almost single-handedly created the myth of radical Musrara. To this day when most outsiders hear our address, this is their first association. The notorious, furious Sa'adia Marciano. When I did finally get around to asking questions and looking into Sa'adia's past, at the library and newspaper archives, I was amazed by the sheer quantity of documents his activities had generated — interviews, photographs, news reports, documentary films, academic articles, leaflets ("Downtrodden Citizen! . . . You are downtrodden not because you were born that way, but because someone is treading on you"), even a Ph.D. dissertation about the day-to-day doings of twenty-two-year-old Sa'adia and his friends. He'd started an adolescent street organizer, leader of a group of poor Musrara kids who'd been in and out of reform school and jail and who were enraged at what they saw as the European-born establishment's contemptuous disregard for pressing social concerns — for *them,* in other words — and wound up a Knesset member, representing a small, left-wing splinter party. (He quit soon after, in a complicated shift of ideological, financial, and power alliances typical of the Israeli parliament.) And even before he'd achieved the unlikely status of public official, he and the others were savvy enough to flamboyantly milk the media and to understand the associative power of the term *Black Panthers.* "We chose that name," Sa'adia explained in one interview, "because we knew that Golda Meir was aware of the American Black Panthers' reputation. We wanted to scare her." (In one classic incident, the Russian-born, American-raised prime minister did in fact sound plenty frightened as she delivered a mousy denunciation of the Panthers after meeting with them. "They are," she said, "not nice.") Nearly every statement the Panthers made, and every defiant display they attempted, became a major headline, in part because Israel a quarter century ago was hardly much more than a big small town, but also because they'd obviously hit a nerve. In many ways, that nerve — ethnic mistrust, economic inequality — remains exposed to this day. And though the Panthers have long since split up, Sa'adia slipped from public view, and the terms of the discussion changed, its pain persists and continues to drive much of the country's internal politics. Looking back, though, through those stacks of brittle clippings, one senses how palpably Sa'adia and his friends must have felt themselves poised on the precipice-edge of the Revolution. One newspaper story, dated September 3, 1971, screamed PANTHERS SURRENDER IN ZION SQUARE, and showed a picture of a pudgy-cheeked Sa'adia, no more than a boy, a cigarette raised in one hand, being grabbed from all sides by a group of older men: He'd staged an illegal demonstration that had given way to a riot, fled underground for several days, then, after alerting the press, given himself up to the authorities in a heat storm of flashbulbs. The caption read "Jerusalem Panther leaders Sa'adia Marciano and Charlie Biton, taken into custody by police detectives in Zion Square . . . Marciano's sweatshirt carries the slogan BY ANY MEANS NECESSARY — MALCOLM X."

Now, at Meir's table, constant reference was made to him as we ate — *Sa'adia said, Sa'adia did, Sa'adia is* — though two hours into the food I began to wonder seriously if he would ever appear. For a few fleeting seconds I even mused that perhaps his coming was just a wishful figment of Meir's imagination. Maybe the hint of his imminent arrival was some sort of practical joke the family played on unwitting Ashkenazi guests. I didn't believe he would come.

We had just finished our dessert when Sa'adia arrived. The older children had run off to play with their cousins and friends in the stairwell; Peter and Meir were leaning, elbows on the table, swapping anecdotes and political talk as Yaffa — now visibly relieved with the intricate choreography of the meal behind her — led me on a glowing tour of the small apartment, showing off the kitchen that she herself had redesigned, with its built-in microwave and shiny black marble counters; the carefully made beds and tidy stacks of toys in the boys' cramped room, a blocked-in balcony; and their own bedroom, Yaffa's perfumes neatly ordered on the dresser, an exercise bike in the corner, for Meir's heart, she explained.

Then in came Sa'adia, without knocking. Groggy from a long evening's nap, he looked like a walking silhouette, with sunken eyes, hollow cheeks, and a skeletal smile. He carried a cell phone in one hand, and the pack of cigarettes in his breast pocket bulged out from his thin frame. After apologizing half a dozen times for being late, he drew the youngest child up on his knee and dug in with his free hand to the full plate Yaffa had rushed to prepare the moment that he entered.

While as guests and hosts we had worked with voluptuous delectation through all the different modes of food, Sa'adia's meal seemed to serve a different purpose altogether. He was hungry in a chronic sense and his sister-in-law didn't ask but just piled high the various courses in overlapping mounds on a wide white plate. He ate fast, without seeming to notice the flavors or colors of the food so much as its filling effect, and as he chewed he talked with the breezy intensity of a man who is used to dominating every conversation in which he participates, using his fork to gesticulate. His banter was friendly, energetic, and not necessarily specific to our presence in the room: I had the sense, in fact, as he outlined his pungent opinions on at least a dozen subjects, that Sa'adia must move from group to group and shadowbox this way. Though I imagined it must be tiring to exist inside that leathery, pugnacious skin, I liked him and admired his indefatigable spikiness. After the initial introductions and chat we learned that he was organizing a concert in honor of an infamously strung-out Yemenite pop singer and Sa'adia's close friend who had hung himself in jail some ten years before. Oh yes, I chimed in, I'd reviewed the singer's movie-biography a few years back.

I stopped myself and asked more cautiously what Sa'adia had thought of the film. It stank, he announced, his mouth half full, a disgrace. I agreed and gave a rough sketch of my critique, as Sa'adia nodded intently, taking in what I said, then went on to detail his firsthand connection to the making of the film — this with a bit of nudging from Meir, who was clearly proud of his older brother and wanted to show him off for the American guests; Sa'adia obliged with a suddenly humble half smile that evolved into a more intent and troubled look as he told in edgy detail the story of how he had served at first as a special adviser on the picture, which he'd considered an important document. But as the project took shape and the director systematically ignored Sa'adia's suggestions, he had grown disgusted and quit. And sure enough, in the end the movie was a hackneyed mess: The director hadn't wanted Sa'adia's opinions or advice so much as his approval, the use of his name. Although his tone retained signs of the itchy agitation I had first noticed when he entered, there was also another, more patiently thinking underside to Sa'adia's talk, an alert and exact kind of calm that informed it, no matter how loud or emphatic he became. When he'd cleared his plate and wiped up the juices with a thick slice of bread, Meir gestured and Yaffa wordlessly filled it again. The late-coming guest of honor dug in once more with the same desperate gusto, as if he hadn't eaten a bite today, or all week, since last Friday night when the same routine had perhaps been enacted.

As he ate this second plate, he promised to get us tickets to the concert, and our talk eased, more freely now, into adjacent topics, including a short movie that Sa'adia once made, with Meir's help. "Get this!" Meir piped up now to explain the plot, which centered on a mental patient named Meir Kahane who is inspired by a visit from the ghost of Adolf Hitler to organize all the other crazies on his ward to storm the Knesset and take over . . . which in turn led to a quieter back-and-forth about America and Israel, where it was that we'd grown up exactly, how we'd come to this country, why we'd decided to stay. Meir and Peter, it turned out, were born in the same year, which at the time seemed jarring to me — though now, thinking back, I cannot say precisely why, or even which of them seemed to me older, just that they held their years so differently, Meir the booming patriarch-to-be, Peter the soft-spoken poet. . . . Did we like it here? Were we satisfied? Meir posed a string of those eternal, impossible questions, to which I know only answers that take shape as other questions, such as *Aren't there problems every-where?* or *Where else would we go?* According to a strange psychological equation, the longer we lived in Jerusalem and the better I understood the place, the less coherent my explanations for my own presence there became. When I'd studied in the city for a semester as a young, inexperienced college student, my first impression had been, in the know-it-all, snap way of so many of my impressions then, clear, unwavering, and unabashedly sentimental. After two decades of living where I didn't quite fit I felt I finally belonged. And though this sense had since been challenged, twisted, tarnished, and made suspect in so many ways, it still (to my amazement, some mornings) more or less held true — though to say so outright after even just a few years spent actually reckoning daily with the place in all its angry contradictions would be partial and misleading. My complaints had grown in direct proportion to my feelings of attachment. The once-exciting newness of it all had given way with time to a more practical, critical engagement. What had been strange was now part of me, or I of it, for better and for worse. This, though, was a necessary part of the acclimation process — the emotional trial by fire that is the hardest thing for visiting Americans, for instance, to understand. *Why do you stay if so much about the place makes you angry?* Attempting to untangle this web of conscious and unconscious "reasons" would be something akin to trying to explain, from the inside out, a loving but tempestuous marriage.

But Meir did not expect an answer so tortured or long-winded. I could, at least, turn his question around and answer a straightforward "Yes, I like it here" if "here" meant the neighborhood, or in fact this dinner table. "I love this place," I announced, which clearly pleased Meir personally. I wasn't trying to act the flatterer, though in that context I realized such a statement would be seen as such: Musrara was nearly their own private property. Earlier in the evening, Meir had proudly announced that their family was among the first two or three to move into the neighborhood, just after the war in 1948. Sa'adia, meanwhile, continued to eat, though his attention seemed to be drifting farther and farther away, or perhaps he was amused in a detached, ironic way by the young American and her apparently unchecked enthusiasm for the streets he knew so well.

It was late — a good sign, declared Meir, who sounded as glad as we felt that the meal had passed with such unexpected pleasure. After we'd said our good-byes and begun the slow stroll home, walking gingerly so as to jar neither our burdened digestive systems nor the tipsy flush of contentment with which the evening had left us, we realized — as an amputee senses a phantom limb perhaps, but without any longing — that once we had passed into their home we'd left our ludicrous fear behind us, as Sa'adia had abandoned his famous hostility and Yaffa had relaxed despite her fragile nerves. Meir was too poised a public presence to let his particular weakness show through but, after his own boisterously thoughtful fashion, he must also have recognized the airy relief that had taken hold as the meal progressed, and that went on lifting us, all the way home, into sleep and through the next day, and the next and onward, as we continued to live in Meir's neighborhood as, somehow — it would always remain so, but now I didn't mind — his welcome guests.

AHMED'S GARDEN

ahmed was balding, with gray stubble on his chin, the inflatable grin of a birthday party clown, and a precarious walk: Despite his grandfatherly years, he waddled as a toddler might after pulling himself to stand and move upright for the first time ever on his own two feet. The baby image was reinforced by the oversized trousers he wore — diaperlike, dirty, and held in place by a thick length of rope that he tied around his belly.

He did not live in the house across the street, but seemed in his own way to belong to it. As far as we could gather, Ahmed had, long ago, before the Jews had settled this part of the neighborhood, laid claim to (owned? rented?) rooms in the large building. Maybe he still did. It was awkward to ask questions, and Ahmed's Hebrew was far too thin for complex response — though even after Peter had begun to learn Arabic and could pour forth a stream of clear, straightforward talk in Ahmed's own language, the old man confined his exchanges with us to his pidgin Hebrew singsong, a series of all-purpose idiomatic phrases he'd picked up, weary intonation included, from the kerchiefed

Moroccan biddies for whom he swept and painted and chased away stray cats. He alternated these expressions freely, no matter what the conversational situation, and smiled with pride as he issued them up, no matter how cranky their flavor: *Not good, not good . . . What can you do? . . . Everything will be all right . . . That's the way it is . . . No problem!* Legal ruminations and detailed family histories were not, evidently, poised on the verbal horizon.

If the official status of his connection to the place was hazy, his feelings seemed quite plain. He was attached to the shady courtyard, the rambling old house across the street, and indeed the whole pitched flagstone alleyway in the selfless, trusting manner of a dog that will walk miles just to be reunited with the lingering trace of a familiar scent. The canine comparison may sound heartless or condescending, but I mean it only in the most objective way and as a means of describing my occasional discomfort at Ahmed's nuzzling determination to serve: When I emerged from our apartment to throw away the kitchen garbage, for instance, he would heave himself up from the stone wall where he was sitting, muttering to himself, seize the bags from my hands, and pad arthritically to the bin down the street. *Let me, let me.* Once when I opened the door to sweep the dust from our front hall, across the threshold, he insisted on taking the broom from me and finishing the job himself, an act I tried and failed to prevent by reaching to grab back the handle. But he was already intently scuttling cobwebs from their corner hideaways; to insist he stop seemed almost mean. He ended up sweeping the entire street.

I cannot know for sure, but I feel close to certain in my bones that Ahmed never had a conscious scheme to return to live in the big stone building across the street — a scheme, that is, which would be reasonable for an ejected tenant to have hatched. While there is always the faint possibility that

Ahmed's smooth brow was hiding vast stores of well-reasoned bitterness that his outward grumbling-but-contented bearing never let slip, his plotting seemed unlikely. He was one of the most practical people I have ever known — a simpleton, he might be called, though there is a nasty edge to this term that doesn't do justice to Ahmed's considerate bearing. He managed to be simple without being a fool. Far from it: He sometimes struck me as the wisest and most rational person on the whole hot-tempered block. That his head seemed almost entirely free of elaborate thoughts did not make him an idiot. If anything, it gave his movements a special, focused tangibility — every impulse was realized in actual terms. If he could not dwell in the house, he seemed to find it sufficient to spend his days in its company, puttering out front, sweeping the outdoor flight of stairs, and heaving groceries for the old women in exchange for a bit of spare change, the broken electronic devices they might be throwing away, a few scraps of stretched-out clothing. Ahmed's interests were financial as much as sentimental, of course, and when he had nothing else to do he would rummage through the garbage bin in search of reusable stuff, fishing out anything glassy, wooden, or made of tin. Then he would add it to one of the growing piles of cryptic detritus he squirreled in the corner of the courtyard and in the basement of the house; these heaps were the only pieces of this property that remained, in actuality, his own. When the stash was large enough, he'd begin to sell off bits and parts to junk dealers around town, though I wondered what the profits could be from this bedraggled collection. The rusting door handles and busted radios, the peeling sides of window frame and halves of cabinet, old toilet bowls, lengths of plastic sheeting — how much could they really be worth? More than a few coins seemed doubtful.

At first I worried for Ahmed, who would not hesitate to plunge his hand into the neighbors' trash, without shame, unknotting the bags to poke his calloused fingers through, then carefully tying them up again and placing them back in the bin. And I worried for us at the same time: Perhaps we were using him, taking advantage? The arrangement seemed crudely colonial. But he appeared so content with his status as caretaker, fix-it man, and honorary neighborhood pack rat that I learned, for his sake, to squelch my fidgety liberal unease. (Once I watched him through the window as he unearthed some slick American magazines I'd tossed out, and his face opened with awe as he flipped backward through that aggressive, corporate shine. For a brief instant, neither illiteracy nor high-gloss advertising seemed to me quite so deplorable.) Who was I to question how Ahmed spent his time? He had chosen to pass his days here and, as it dawned on me gradually, he also had another, more important role to play — as the garden's guardian angel.

※❖❖※

There hadn't been a garden when we came to live on the street, just as at first Ahmed's presence had not registered in any special way: He passed through once every couple of weeks, collected a few junky odds and ends in a wilted burlap sack, performed a small chore for one of the grandmothers, and moved on. His stronger link to the place only asserted itself later, in a slightly mysterious way, after Peter had won the approval of the wary neighbors and worked hard, to their bafflement but apparent satisfaction, to clear away the heaps of wooden planks and piles of pipe that had been gathering for years in the middle of the courtyard opposite us.

Obviously the space had once contained a fine Arab garden — it was designed for this purpose, with its wide-open central square plot, shoe-heel-smoothed flagstone path, stately stone wall, and the trees. Four tall, sparrow-filled cypresses, an unpruned pomegranate, and a rangy olive were all that remained of the pre-State *bustan*. But the garden itself was a ghost, and the other fruit trees and sweet-smelling climbers I imagined once flourishing there had long since withered and vanished, the rocky soil hardened and gone to hip-high weed. The place was far from quaint in its dilapidation, though. Amid the bursts of thistle, caper, dandelion, and scraggly grass there were broken bottles and piles of cat dung, bags of rotting trash: The place was a sort of permanent eyesore that the old-timers had stopped noticing, even after they had gone to great, costly lengths to overhaul their own homes, retiling floors and installing new kitchens, which they kept hysterically clean. Nothing would grow there, they warned us when we asked if we might plant a few saplings. "The soil is dead." But our apartment looked right out onto this dump, and Peter had decided, even before we'd moved in, to restore the garden to its rightful place, and to fill our windows with color. A young couple, both musicians — Yona, French and softly owlish, and his wife, Vered, an Israeli with a thick, rich speaking voice and throaty laugh that had a faint but appealing foreign ring — lived with their new baby in one of the apartments on the top floor, and they had agreed to help, which was fortunate. The garden plot was not our property and the few days they spent, helping drag away rocks and splintery boards, made the project legitimate, and removed any stigma of Manifest Destiny on our part.

But Peter did the bulk of the work himself, while I shuttled trash bags and glasses of water and offered occasional advice. First he hauled garbage, then dug out and cleared the jagged chunks of chalky stone that were so abundant they seemed almost to breed there. Next he weeded, then began the slow process of turning the soil. It hadn't been touched since 1948, as one of the old men who lived in the house announced with an odd sort of pride. A watery-eyed pensioner who wore a pancake beret pulled tight over his scalp and a wool scarf knotted at his throat no matter the weather, he was quietly thrilled that Peter had decided to plant a garden — this plan seemed to fulfill some long-held fantasy he'd harbored in secret but had been unable, for whatever reason, to realize himself — and each time he passed my husband at work, he would bless him a dozen times, once for every other step of his inching staircase ascent. The man's grown son, meanwhile, a loudly dim-witted waiter at an overrated hummus joint downtown, and an infamous fan of the city's favorite soccer team, also lived in the house and seemed a bit jealous of the attention and praise his father lavished on this green-thumbed, fair-haired American interloper, in direct contrast to the disgusted shouts the father reserved for his son, and vice versa. So the younger man eagerly approached Peter with his *own* plan to build a special tiled barbecue deck in the back corner of the garden. He would also be happy to pay "some Arab" to cut down the century-old cypress trees — which, he reminded the new-immigrant gardener in the confident tones of a seasoned veteran, only made dirt and drank up all the water in the ground. Peter managed to talk him gently out of both of these dreadful plans and made his peace with Shlomi's stubborn determination to repeatedly chop down the hearty tree of heaven that had sprouted up without coaxing in the back corner of the garden. It was Keystone Kop–comical to watch this battle between the slow, stupid man and the quick, clever plant: Shlomi was no match for the determined weed-tree, which grew even faster and fuller after each of his klutzy assaults. He eventually gave up, and the tree grew to tower over the garden.

When the soil was ready, we began to make afternoon taxi runs to the local nurseries where the tanned workers — who all seemed temperamentally quite similar, easygoing and unruffled as bass guitar players in their flappy flannel shirts — soon knew us by name and would leave us alone to wander and choose what we wanted from the blooming rows. In stages throughout that first growing year, we planted a ring of fruit trees (loquat, apricot, and lemon) as well as yellow and white jasmine, a dainty white starburst climber called a solanum, or potato vine, magenta bougainvillea, oleander in three different shades, geranium, and a cestrum bush — a spurting, purple-flowered effusion of green that we'd never noticed before but recognized immediately when we saw it later at the Alhambra. There it grew dense and high as a great waterfall, flowing backward and up.

Ahmed's presence started to sink in sometime during the garden's second season, when the plants had begun to take root but hadn't yet really flourished, and at first his being there didn't seem to make a great difference. He would putter around the edge of the trees (to which, by then, we'd added two graceful young olives and another pomegranate), sweeping the walkway, stooping to scoop up trash, pulling grass from between the stones of the streetside wall, where it grew like bushy mortar. Then he quietly eased himself into closer involvement with the daily business of maintaining the garden, rigging a crude but effective stake of iron pipe for one of the oleanders that leaned too far to the left, arranging a border of spare stones around the nearly dead rosebush he'd rescued from someone's trash bin and miraculously nursed back to life. He had a special sense for finding the handiness inherent in *all* materials, no matter how artificial, and would anchor a tilting bush to a tin curtain rod with a large plastic bag, or use a length of withered polyester yarn to guide a climbing plant over the wall. Twisted bits of electrical wire turned up along the stair's banister, where they held the jasmine in place. Without saying a word, then, he began to weed — no small job, since the soil had responded immediately to being turned and watered, and an entire lawn of stubbly new nettles, clover, and rough grass had sprung up already, replacing the taller growth that Peter had cleared. When Ahmed was through removing all this unwanted green, he would rake in orderly lines, leaving the place looking elegant and cooler in its own spreading shade.

The plants began to respond to his touch, and though some of this was fussing that Peter himself could have done (and some of it he did; twice a week in summertime I would heave the hose over our porch wall and across the street, where he was waiting to douse the garden with its only source of dry-season water) and other progress was due to the passing of time and the gradual unfurling of stronger roots and branches — Ahmed brought something else to the garden, with his constant clearing, attending, adjusting, minding. I hesitate to name this thing, for I know that in its essence it has no satisfactory title, and that one walks a dangerous minefield of cliché when one mentions the simple happy native at work in the simple happy garden. But there is no getting around the fact that Ahmed, in his execution of these thousand tiny, spontaneous chores, had a weird, almost magical influence on the growth of the trees and flowers. Without coaxing, for instance, a bright pink hollyhock popped from the "dead" earth sometime just after Ahmed appeared, and it grew within weeks to his own height (small for a man, huge for a flower): the Jack-and-the-Beanstalk scale of the plant and its sudden appearance suggested enchantment, its seed blown in on a strange, knowing wind. And soon other shoots burst into fairy-tale bloom. . . .

There was, in fact, nothing self-conscious or even *intentional* about his relationship to the garden. If anything, he was unaware of his special connection and simply went about his business, performing the necessary tasks with the same lack of pretense that most of us use to breathe or walk. He seemed, too, impervious to insult. After he'd labored for hours and hours yanking out weeds, and spent several lengthy days erecting a lopsided green chicken-wire fence on one side, to keep the puppy of the downstairs tenant from escaping, he began to fill a plastic pail with olives from the gnarly adult tree. His picking also seemed an almost-necessary reaction to harvest-time, a kind of innate awareness on his part of the shape of the seasons: When the olives were ripe, one must gather them, of course, to cure and eat over the next year or to sell raw on the street for a few more coins. But another neighbor, Hannah, recently widowed and by nature a mild crank, yelled at him and ordered him to stop. The olives belonged to the whole neighborhood, she insisted, on principle — though, as became plain, she had no intention of gathering the olives herself. (No one did, in fact, and to my somewhat lazy dismay the lot of them dropped to the ground or wrinkled bitterly right on the tree.) So Ahmed shook his head and muttered faint curses under his breath, then shrugged and returned to the fence, which needed straightening.

Later, when the garden was already established as a living, thriving fact, Ahmed disappeared. For several months running, there was no sign of him. The weeds grew thick without him, and we began to worry, not for the plants, but for Ahmed: Taking off wasn't like him. He'd seemed to need to putter in the garden several times a week, for his peace of mind, if not for the measly hand-out he got for his various labors. He wouldn't just abandon his work (not to mention his carefully stacked junk heaps) like that, without warning. Something must be wrong. Peter asked Shlomi, did he know what had happened? And Shlomi answered with a terrible, indifferent shrug, "To the Arab? Who knows? Maybe he died."

There was nothing we could do, no way to trace Ahmed — whose comings and goings had always seemed such a given that I'd never really thought to question irrelevant details like his last name or precise address. Peter set to work weeding the garden himself, and while the plants continued to grow and to bloom, it seemed to me (or was I imagining?) that the trees and climbing flowers had noticed Ahmed's absence, and were somehow sadder for it, a little droopy, their colors a shade less intense.

But eventually Ahmed did return, with a hacking cough and a newly crooked gait. He was wearing a knitted winter hat in summertime; he limped. Hearing his noisy, phlegmy approach, we went outside to say hello and he greeted us right off with a typically blustery-but-resigned, monosyllabic account of where he'd been. A few months ago, two blocks away, he was hit by a car and left there, in the road. No one helped him. The invisible man. "Teeth —" he indicated with a sweep of the hand, "all on the ground." He'd been in the hospital for weeks and, as if his hit-and-run-inflicted wounds weren't enough, he had come down with pneumonia. "What can you do?" he sighed loudly, already turning to rifle through one of his piles.

Remarkably enough, given the injuries he'd suffered, of both a physical and emotional sort (he had, he said, been forced to lie in the road in a pool of his own blood and incisors for "a long time" before someone came to his rescue: minutes? hours? I wondered with a flinch), Ahmed didn't seem especially distressed. He continued to mutter to himself and to sort through the trash and tie up the red roses with spare bits of wire. We gave him some money, and he put it in his pocket with a satisfied grin and one of his pet formulas, "Thank you *very very* much. Everything will be all right," he would say when we slipped him a bill, though he made it clear that what he'd really like was clothing — any old pants, sweaters, or, best of all, shoes, we could spare. "Thank you *very very* much. Everything will be all right."

This was not, though, the last of his disappearances. A while after his accident and recovery, he vanished yet again. And again we asked ourselves, What happened? Was he ill once more or had something inside of him snapped as a result of his wounds and the way he'd been ignored by those cars speeding by? Or was there some other reason for his absence? He never returned to explain. The last time I saw Ahmed was the first time I ever saw him truly upset: He was sitting on a stoop at the bottom of our street, and he seemed to me to be sobbing. I approached him and asked what was wrong. "Son of a bitch, son of a bitch," he kept saying. He was clutching his burlap sack and his eyes were wet, though I do not know if he was crying or sick. He kept coughing. "Son of a bitch. All day, I work all day. They pay five shekel, *chamsa* shekel, *ya ben zona.*" He slipped into Arabic numbers but stuck to Hebrew curses. He did not appear to be angry at me, but hurt by the way he'd been used by our neighbors. And while it is tempting to assign his tears to a sudden awareness of the larger, longer, deeper injustice of his situation — here he was, an impoverished Palestinian, swabbing for pennies the once-Arab-owned steps of the Jews' house — that does not seem right: Ahmed was, again, very practical in his complaints. Something particular had happened that day and it had upset him profoundly. What? "*Chamsa* shekel, son of a bitch . . ." When I tried to offer help and clarify what exactly had gone on (five shekels, about $1.25 at the time, was indeed an offensively minuscule sum to pay for a full day's work, which should have brought him one hundred shekels at the very least), he looked up but right through me, without answering, then finally propped himself to standing and walked away, shaking his head, wiping his eyes, coughing, cursing.

Chronologically at least, that was my final glimpse of Ahmed, though another image lingered on, long after he departed and Shlomi hauled away his precious trash collection with much angry fanfare at seven o'clock one morning, cursing to their baffled faces the Ethiopian neighbors for not lending a hand: "They're worse than the Arabs." That other picture of Ahmed hovered in my field of vision, as a sort of holographic flicker, whenever I looked out across the street, through the window, and this shadowy sight almost convinced me that he was — or his spirit was — still somehow protecting the plants he had once tended in person with such unstinting love. . . .

At the end of the day, an average day, after he'd made sure that every bush and vine was solidly propped, the undergrowth cleared, and the lot's bare sandy patches neatly smoothed across, Ahmed would finally allow himself to slow down. With a heavy sigh he would lower his tired frame onto an upholstered footrest that he'd salvaged, tattered and wobbly, from yet another garbage bin and placed like a low throne at the center of the plot. One hand slung across his knee, the other holding his small wooden pipe, he would sit, taking silent puffs, leaning forward, at last at peace in his garden.

CLOSE BRUSH

ⅩⅩⅩⅩⅩⅩⅩⅩⅩⅩⅩⅩⅩⅩⅩⅩⅩⅩ

we both recognized the sinister drone of the buzz saw the instant it started, though a few more moments passed before we traced its exact origin. The stone walls of the nearby houses played tricks with the din, and the echo of the blade's harsh ring first sent us scrambling downhill instead of up, in search of the source. By now we knew that sound and its meaning all too well. In just a few months' time, two of the neighborhood's oldest and loveliest trees had been hacked down to the strains of that same vile rattle. First, the tallest pine in the municipal garden was felled in minutes flat, too abruptly for us to do anything but mourn it. The man we knew was responsible — he had recently attached a huge, garish balcony to his top-floor apartment and cleared the tree to allow an unobstructed eastern view — denied it with a snide shrug, not worth challenging. The tree was already reduced to a stump and, we realized, no argument would bring it back.

Then, by cruel coincidence, on the same day Rafi's mother slipped out of her coma and into death at the Gates of Justice hospital, another neighbor began his attack on the grand eucalyptus whose dipping and swishing I had attended so raptly from the bedroom window on Daniel Street, and whose gentle undulations had served as a familiar, dynamic backdrop to the view from our newer porch. The dead woman, too, had spent every afternoon since I had known her — and probably for several decades before — sitting on her balcony, staring off in the direction of the tree. Now, in just a few days' time, both it and she would be gone forever. When we realized what was happening, Peter called the parks department's hot line (lukewarm was more like it), and waited on the phone as a string of sleepy-sounding operators transferred him here, and then there and around again, through a loop of other operators, who each listened in turn to his complaint, then mumbled "just a minute" or yawned at him to "wait" then switched him elsewhere, each passing of the bureaucratic buck punctuated by a blast of cheerful Muzak. Meanwhile, in the background, the saw groaned on. When finally he reached the appropriate department and explained one more time about the eucalyptus, the woman on the other end grumbled that she would have to check the file, this might take some time. He should call back in half an hour. And when he did, it was only to learn that all was legal. There was nothing we could do. The man did have a year-old permit that allowed him to cut down the tree: The roots might damage his house's foundations, the clerk read from the form. And, besides, the higher branches stood in the way of low-flying planes. Too dismayed to laugh out loud, Peter hung up the phone and we were forced to listen to that taunting metallic death knell for a full week afterward, as the self-appointed lumberjack and his helper chopped, meter by meter, down to the base of the tree. When they finished, the landscape had a hole in it, a terrible dead space in the air where that constant green flutter ought to be. This, though, was a weird, almost wraithlike phenomenon that seemed even to apply to the cypress that had once, we had heard, existed near the edge of our porch, before another neighbor "helped" it to come down. He began quietly to uproot it — "trees make dirt," we were told, yet again, in terse explanation for the perceived need to remove from the local landscape as much greenery as possible — and then when the once-in-a-decade blizzard came, used the "dangerous" weight of the snow as an excuse to fell the tree. Although I'd never seen that cypress, I could sometimes swear I felt its absent shade, heard its invisible swish in the wind.

This time we had advance warning. About a week before, Peter had happened upon a "little ape of a man," as he unapologetically dubbed him, with a long black beard and blue cap who had crawled high up into the stocky eucalyptus that sat a few yards from the fresh pine stump in the municipal garden, and was attempting to amputate one of the thickest branches with his puny handsaw. Peter had called to the man to ask him what he was doing and why. The man cursed him and told him to *Mind your own business* and *Get lost,* till Peter yelled louder and threatened to call the cops. (On paper, at least, cutting down trees without permission is a criminal offense in Jerusalem.) Then the man had descended, his face hot, eyes and neck veins popping, and pushed Peter in the chest as he screamed at the top of his lungs, "WHO ARE YOU? YOU'RE NOT EVEN A JEW!" (Meaning he didn't dress in the standard religious black-and-white uniform and grow his sidelocks long — or, worse still and not altogether improbable, given Peter's tough-to-place accent — he might be a half-breed, heathen Russian, a devoted sausage eater!) Realizing he had locked horns with a lunatic, Peter turned to go. The man abandoned his work soon after.

But now a brief, fruitless trip downhill made it clear that the buzz saw was humming from the very same tree. I dispatched myself to go investigate while Peter dialed the police and the parks department, yet again. On my way out the door, I grabbed a book — a cookbook, it turned out, from which I would pretend to study recipes for lentil soup with melon and fish baked in salt as I spied and awaited the squad car — and, sure enough, there in the tree was a short bearded man who matched Peter's monkeyish description: He had a compact body, long swinging arms, and the telltale cornflower cap. As he talked to himself, the edges of his mouth drooped buffoon-ishly and his nostrils swelled and shrunk, swelled and shrunk like a set of cartoon bellows. And though his bearing was some-how comic — his grotesquely disproportionate features sug-gested a crayon drawing rendered by a small child — there was nothing even vaguely funny about the destruction he had already accomplished. He had wiggled into the top part of the eucalyptus and was breathing heavily as he heaved all his weight at one sturdy bough. The branch was far too massive for his cheap hand tools, which he had inadvertently contrived, in the course of just a few minutes, to lodge deep into the wood. Abandoning the dulled spikes and pickax there for the time being, he'd now moved on to an electric saw and he seemed mad, even vindictive, determined to injure the tree for the losses it had caused him. And sure enough, as he shoved the blade back and forth, swearing and grunting loudly, he managed quite efficiently — if that is the word for the speedy execution of such slipshod butchery — to seriously mangle the tree.

What could I do? I paced beneath him with my cookbook, round and round the trunk, and even contemplated snatching his Charlie-the-tramp-like satchel, which rested on the ground nearby. If he scrambled down to get the bag back I could spare the tree further damage before the police came. But the thought of this little man pushing *me* in the chest and shrieking racial epithets was more than I could bear. (He was slight but looked strong, agitated, and definitely crazy enough to hurt me.) And if the police arrived to discover that I had stolen his belongings, things might get messy. . . . So I continued to pace, round the trunk, and round. The man ignored me as he sent rough chunks of wood crashing down on the bushes below.

Meanwhile, Nehama, our former neighbor, had appeared in a floor-length plush housedress and slippers on her balcony and was taking in the scene through what looked to me from a distance like a suspicious squint. "Leave him be," she called out to me with a wary smile and warning tone. "He's just earning a little money."

"But the *tree* . . ." I attempted, rather feebly, as several of the students from the yeshiva right beside the eucalyptus emerged to smoke cigarettes, eye me, and flamboyantly greet the small bearded man, whom, I soon realized, they themselves had hired to perform their illegal tree-slaughter. Now they were determined to protect him from a hard-hearted, nature-loving outsider like me.

This yeshiva, it ought to be said, existed at the very epicenter of the neighborhood as both a literal and figurative black hole. It was a study house for the newly religious, and most of the men who lived and learned the fundamentals of Jewish law there had a distractedly unkempt and tentative look about them, as if they were in hiding. They called themselves penitents but most wore the long, ill-fitting dark coats, the wide-brimmed hats, and scruffy beards of ultra-Orthodoxy as a kind of defensive costume, a dare to those who would question their spiritual superiority. A sloppy anger emanated from the place. Many of the students had, at some point in their former lives, spent time in prison or reform school, though few seemed like serious felons: Their demeanor suggested small fry, occasional crime. I imagined most had been petty crooks, amateur drug dealers, participants in yelling matches that had unexpectedly turned bloody. Perhaps they were cat burglars. Now that they were saved (or, as the Hebrew phrase would have it, they had "returned with the answer"), they parked their cars at crowded angles all along the garden path and tossed their towels from the ritual bath to dry over the green plastic tarp they had slung crookedly around the front courtyard, built in the hostile haste that usually signaled illegal construction. And their sneering contempt for everyone who was not of their kind — that is, Jewish, male, religious, right wing, and dark-skinned — made me walk faster when I passed their courtyard. There was something sordid and aggressive about their collective gaze: Aside from the periods they had spent behind bars, these men had lived "outside," without such strict rules about purity and the separation of the sexes, and while they might adhere now to a prudery they considered heaven-sent, they hadn't adjusted their bald habit of staring. If anything, I sensed that the laws they had recently learned on the subject gave them the feeling of lecherous entitlement, especially where secular women in short skirts were concerned. Officially, at least, they fancied themselves above "base" passions, and so deemed it kosher to ogle all they liked. *Their* women knew to dress modestly.

Unfortunately, on this particular summer day, I had burst out of the house in my T-shirt and thin cotton skirt without thinking. And now, as a few of them emerged from the study house to see what was going on in the tree and to argue (they looked ready to argue at all times), they didn't hesitate to address their remarks, in a creepy, unblinking way, directly at my bare legs. I clutched the cookbook closer to my chest and started to pace. "What's with you?" one of them snorted. "It's not a fruit tree."

"What?" I snapped back, a bit too forcefully. "It's a *tree* — he's destroying the tree."

"But it's only forbidden to cut down fruit trees," explained the smug man who stood before me, broadly scratching his pot-belly. "It's written."

"You're a religious man —" I said, not thinking too clearly and sputtering a bit as the tree chunks continued to litter down behind me. "He's killing the tree. It's a kind of murder, no? Don't you *see*?"

Potbelly was amused by my agitated tone, and he grinned as he called up to the man in the tree "*Yosef!* She says you're a murderer!" There were chuckles all around, a bit of noisy whispering, and then the monkey man, Yosef, inched back down the tree. Aggressively avoiding eye contact with me, he began to make the rounds of his smirking supporters, shaking hands with each of the onlookers who had gathered to rally around him and cast shifty looks in my direction. One slapped him on the back, another offered him a cigarette, and yet another put his arm around the little man and mumbled in his ear. With this, he began to look a bit anxious. His face flushed to angry pink, he muttered something harsh-sounding just under his breath, then let the mumbler steer him away from the tree and me, and toward the public housing projects below. The cue had been given: As the two disappeared into a sea of concrete, the other yeshiva students dispersed and I was left alone with the tools and the wounded tree.

At this point, the police pulled up. The officers looked tired and a little bit bored by my story, which only made me more defiant as I described the man, showed them his abandoned tools, and gestured in the approximate direction toward which he'd fled. One of them began a strolling search for the missing perpetrator while the other stayed to radio dispatch. By this time, the presence of the squad car in the middle of the garden had created a small stir. A group of preteen punks with buzz cuts had gathered on their bicycles to witness an arrest. Nehama had descended to the street, in full naptime regalia, and was talking in muted, conspiratorial tones with a few of the yeshiva students who had reemerged from their fortress-lair and now stood watching at a curious remove. *"Mizken,"* she said, clicking her tongue when I approached her, "poor thing . . . he's just doing his job. He doesn't have anything, it's just a job. Poor thing . . ." she began again, and though I tried once more to defend the tree itself as a "poor thing," I understood as I spoke that I had drifted into waters much deeper and murkier than I had first realized when I set forth. Not only was my basic, arboreal concern completely alien to these parts, but my defense of the tree was viewed by Nehama as a direct assault on other, more essential values. In her mind, I could see, there was a selfish, cold, even un-Jewish aspect both to my feeling for the tree and my method of handling the problem. Calling the police was a last resort, to be taken only in extreme, life-threatening instances, which the cutting down of a mute evergreen most certainly was not, to her mind: better to bellow and carry on than involve officials who didn't, anyway, have to live day in day out with the people next door and who didn't subscribe to the somewhat faulty local logic that said there was no problem, major or minor, that couldn't be solved by just screaming loudly enough. Now, it was clear, the struggle for the future of this eucalyptus was about to metamorphose into a showdown of nasty, racial sorts — which was the very last thing I'd ever wanted when I set out to save a tree that had, in fact, stood guard at the neighborhood's center long before my own pale-skinned arrival. About then, Peter wandered up cautiously from our street and a few minutes later Nomi, our widowed jeweler-neighbor, also passed by and stopped to commiserate, an unfortunate coincidence that worked to further emphasize the us–them aspect of the standoff taking ugly shape around the base of the tree.

For all its apparent serenity, the municipal garden had for some time now been associated in my mind with a slow-boiling sort of ethnic hatred. Abed, the soft-spoken Palestinian gardener who had cared with such patience for the plumbago and ole-

ander there, had recently quit — driven away by a combination
of factors, some of which he explained to Peter in staccato
Hebrew (the solitary weeding, watering, pruning made him
lonely, he said; he preferred to work with a crew). Then, to top
it all off, a group of neighborhood children had started a horrible game of taunting Abed — jumping on his water hose, calling out names, and yanking up the flowers he'd just planted.
Instead of fighting them off, he had left as soon as the insults
began, clenching his jaw and requesting a transfer. He preferred
to work in Arab East Jerusalem, no matter if the job of gardener there entailed more garbage detail, less plant maintenance. He was understandably hurt at the way these brats had
treated him, though he remained friendly toward us, far too
polite and dignified to ever stop smiling when we saw him later
in the East, and he recounted the awful story.

The yeshiva students hadn't, it was true, been directly
involved in Abed's leaving, but I couldn't help thinking that
their rude proximity had also made him uneasy. Theirs was a
noisy, sprawling presence at the garden's center. They seemed to
need to assert their dominance by defying nature, manhandling
it — the delicate almond tree right in front of their door, for
instance, became a coatrack, over which they'd drape their
wilted clothing — and while they shared with Abed the strict
tendencies of the Orthodox (at his cue from the muezzin, he
would stop work at regular intervals to pray on a small cardboard mat), his bearing was quite the opposite of theirs: contained, businesslike, almost mute.

Just as I began to think in horror of how Abed would have
responded to the vision of the ax tip jammed into the flesh of
the tree, a pickup truck stenciled with the municipal parks
department logo pulled up, bearing Abed's replacement, sullen
as always in his green uniform. A very young man, a boy really,
with a molting mustache, thick glasses, and a blank look, he'd

let the garden wither and scorch since Abed had left — whether in conscious defiance or mere laziness, I could not say. He was accompanied by a Jewish supervisor, a middle-aged Yemenite with a swarthy face, a Hawaiian shirt unbuttoned to his ample paunch, and a pair of worn sandals. In just a few seconds, this man — a savior of exhausted-looking sorts — had already grasped what was happening and taken stern control. "Who is responsible for this?" he asked, staring at the yeshiva students, who had grown suspiciously silent and averted their gaze the moment he had stepped from the truck. His skin was several shades darker than that of the darkest of them, and in a certain, horrible sense, all he needed to do to diffuse the feverish racial tension that had seized this ragtag group was stand there, hands on hips, in front of the tree whose presence he'd come to defend, showing off his coffee-brown pigment.

"Whose tools are these?" No one spoke. "*Whose . . . tools . . . are . . . these?*" he asked again, softly, this time looking harder at each of the black-hatted men in turn. One of them, a gangly jokester with a wiry beard, sneered and muttered something to his friend beside him, at which the supervisor turned to face him, irritated but restrained, formal in a faintly ironic way. "Is this funny? Maybe you, sir, can tell me something about what's going on here."

And before the Jokester was forced to lie and claim his ignorance, Yosef the monkey man appeared, huffing and puffing and obviously upset as he sweated up the hill. Ignoring the police, the parks official, the gardener, and the curious crowd that had gathered, he approached his satchel and began the rather clownish task of trying to collect nonchalantly the few remaining tools that he hadn't lodged in the tree.

"Excuse me." The supervisor continued to speak in the same measured tones. "But are these your things? What are you doing to this tree? You know there are fines for damaging trees." At the panic-stricken look that Yosef gave his own shoes, the supervisor's voice grew softer. "Who hired you to do this?"

Without any warning, Yosef began to scream in Hebrew and curse in Arabic, and charged the dark-skinned official, head-first, as if preparing to butt him with his blue cap. "NO ONE HIRED ME, *your mother's a whore,* LEAVE ME ALONE!" The yeshiva toughs jumped to hold him back.

The supervisor blinked and shifted his weight, nonplused. "Who . . . hired . . . you . . . to . . . do . . . this?"

"Your sister's a cunt, you son of a whore —"

"Leave him alone," the Jokester dove in, too insistently. "He didn't do anything." Catching himself sounding a bit overinvolved, he gave a little, helpless shrug, as if daring the supervisor to bully *him* instead of the runtish man.

"Maybe *you* know something, then, if you're so sure you know what he did or didn't do." The Jokester shrugged again, in unmasked mockery, and as the supervisor turned his gaze back to Yosef to check his reaction, the little man looked ready to burst into terrified tears.

His face grew still redder and now he began to plead in a shameless, whispery way, stepping up to stand much too close to the official, lifting his face upward to beg: "Let me go. Just forget about the tree." The supervisor sighed wearily, then moved off to get some air and signal the police to leave. Their threatening presence wasn't helping any and had only served, it seemed, to set the little man off on his neurotic jag.

This back-and-forth continued for some time, with the park supervisor posing patient questions and even offering the shaken man gardening work at City Hall if he would point a finger at the person who'd paid him. But he continued to refuse and pounced frequently from one aggravated state to the next (he cowered, he screamed, he pleaded, he cursed). At the same time, the yeshiva students either paced the perimeter or defended the accused in noncommittal terms called out from the sidelines, while other onlookers — especially Nehama — piped up often to offer support for the little man's actions. The branch, she insisted, *looked* sturdy, but who knew? It might fall down one day and hurt the children playing below. *Now* it might fall down, I tried to counter. Now that he had severed its base from the trunk and left it to dangle it was dangerous. It had been fine before he came along. *But the children!* she insisted in turn, and I knew it was best for me just to shut up: No matter the contentious subject of discussion (chemical warfare, daylight saving time, terrorism, the water supply), this inevitable *but-the-children* line of reasoning always stood as a dead end of incontestible sorts. Rhetorically, at least, the children of Israel were the be-all and end-all, the altar on which every shard of reason, calm, and self-respect could be sacrificed without apology or shame. I bit my tongue and looked up at the poor orphaned branch, left half-attached in painful suspension over the tiny park, where in actuality few children ever played.

Peter, at the same time, exchanged charged words with the Jokester, who was a bumbling but determined liar. By now his agitated interjections made it plain that *he* was the one who had personally hired the man to do his tree chopping and though he wasn't prepared to step up and take responsibility for the crime, he felt he could not abandon the little man at the height of his interrogation. (It wasn't pure altruism that kept him there, though. He seemed nervous that Yosef might, with his departure, start to name names.) The monkey man wasn't much good at dissembling either, and as he trembled he watched the Jokester out of the corner of his rapidly blinking eye, making it clear once and for all that he trembled in terror not of the police but of his patron, who was twice his size and boss of the block. He might explode if accused, and would certainly never *ever* find Yosef another odd job again.

But the scared little man need not have worried. The Jokester had already redirected his nervous energy and was anxiously attempting to aggravate my husband. Peter had just stated with an exotic sort of placidity that he knew the man was lying; he ought to stop faking and admit what he had done. His honor and honesty challenged in such a cool, apparently unbothered manner by a hatless American, the Jokester looked baffled. When your opponent screamed, it was obvious what to do: You screamed back and threatened him physically. But when faced with this understated accusation, the other man looked lost, almost saddened by Peter's mild tone. He tried, feebly, to start a fight on moral grounds, a kind of Talmudic tug-of-war, as if he thought he might goad Peter into anger by interjecting a few of the more sophisticated argumentative strategies he'd just picked up at the yeshiva. "You — you just come in here and start making accusations. What do you care? What do you know? It's not *your* tree. This man was just trying to earn a little money, so someone paid him to work. It's between the two of them. You don't know anything about this. And even if you did, you'd see *I* know nothing, *I* didn't do anything. I was just sitting inside, minding my own business, when I heard all the noise you were making out here. What's it to you?"

Getting no response whatsoever from Peter, who merely stood there, staring back, the Jokester began to get frantic and protest too much, his voice growing louder. "Who are *you* to start calling *me* a liar? Do you know me? NO. And this tree is none of your business anyway. Who do you think you ARE? I am NOT a LIAR." With this last, stentorian proclamation, which had a new and slightly desperate ring, he turned his gaze away from that of the supervisor — who had fixed him now in a knowing, inescapable, entirely native way — and sighed, apparently conceding a certain grudging guilt.

After this explosion, the fireworks fizzled out. The yeshiva boys scattered; the Jokester stomped off; the punks got bored and rode away; Nehama smiled at us at the conclusion of another afternoon's entertainment and excused herself to go prepare dinner; the monkey man calmed slightly as the supervisor talked to him in the low, even tones that one uses to quiet a crying child (apparently some private deal had been reached); and we mumbled our thanks to the parks official then made our way back home, too exhausted by the whole elaborate jousting match to fret much more about the tree's future, which we'd tried our hardest to secure. Its fate was now out of our hands.

In the months following, after Yosef reclaimed his tools and disappeared, and the park returned to its former overgrown state, the episode with the tree was almost forgotten. The eucalyptus was safe for the time being, and only two small signs of the incident remained. First of all, the Jokester, recognizing he had been caught in a lie, turned into a perfect gentleman around both of us — bowing gallantly and asking about our health each time we passed him wandering the street with his brutish entourage, or standing around the counter at Meir's, where he was a regular whiskey-sipper and where, I imagined, our friend the grocer may well have set him straight about the venality of *those stinking Ashkenazis*. The Jokester was especially polite and forthcoming when he saw us inside Meir's store.

Then the hacked branch itself sprouted a feathery burst of new, pale leaves, which seemed to emerge from the splintered wood as a sweetly comic footnote to the whole obnoxious episode. As far as the tree was concerned, the close brush with the buzz saw had been nothing more traumatic than an invitation to put forth fresh foliage. Like new hair growing out beneath a bad dye job, this young effusion was softer and several shades lighter than the older, tougher green, and soon covered the entire battered branch-stump with its gentle swaying.

HERE IS A PICTURE YOU
WILL FIND UNFORGETTABLE

(OR: HOW GREEN WAS MY VALLEY)

as the pivot point of a compass, our street
in Musrara was the axis around which all my rovings through
the city took shape. We did not have or want a car, so to make
my way out of the neighborhood, I would turn right at our
doorstep, pass with a mutual nod the ponytailed mothers who
smoked and gabbed as their children
played in the paved lot above, cut up the
path through the garden surrounding the
yeshiva, then venture the alley of a staircase that ran between a tall stone house
and quiet Ethiopian bodega. Percussive
music played softly from a tape deck
there, while the young owner and his
friends sat on plastic chairs, talking and
sipping beer beneath a national-airline-
styled poster of a toothless old black man,
swathed in flowing robes, and another, of
Michael Jackson.

There was always a hush around this
passage, which marked the line between the relative pedestrian
calm of the park and the main thoroughfare above, where Meir's
grocery store sat, beside Mahlouf's ragtag vegetable stand and
Moshe's newspaper-and-lottery-ticket kiosk, actually a small
stone lean-to attached to his own ground-floor apartment.

MARCEL'S KIOSK
MORE MILLIONAIRES IN THE LOTTO

declared the candy-corn-colored awning provided by his sponsor, though I never heard a soul call Moshe or his business by this other, Francophone name, nor had anyone, so far as I knew, ever become an overnight fat cat by means of a ticket purchased there. Throughout the week I might stop in to buy a few tomatoes from Mahlouf or a Hebrew paper from Moshe, but on Fridays I made my rounds, visiting Meir's store first for my usual milk-bread-cheese-juice supplies, next moving on to Mahlouf's for a few potatoes or onions, then dragging my purchases into Moshe's to collect the weekend paper he'd begun to hold for me right after we moved in, without my ever asking. The instant he saw me coming, he would waddle inside from his outdoor-bench post to assemble the appropriate papers from the eight or so different choices.

With his checked cap tipped over his salt-and-pepper hair, his studious wire-framed glasses, round belly, and the plastic beach thongs he wore throughout spring, summer, and as long into fall as the temperature would allow, his pudgy bare toes poking out, there was something a touch farcical about Moshe's proportions. He had, too, the timing of a natural comedian, though he never cracked more than the faintest smile and would deliver all his silliest comments with the same slightly offended glare, sometimes punctuated by an otherwise-straight-faced wink. High up on the wall, above the piles of basic food items he stocked and the fluorescent lotto signs announcing the size of the week's jackpot in both so-called and actual Arabic numerals (20 and ٢٠), hung several portraits of a much younger Moshe. Two were ink drawings of the sort that may be commissioned and executed spontaneously from street artists midsummer in the main plazas of most European capitals, and neither really looked like Moshe, but they did at least capture something of his stubborn, forward-thrust jaw and somber brow. Although he may have been posing so sternly in the same ironical way that he executed most every task (scolding his adolescent grandson; trading friendly insults with Ali, the fix-it man, who stopped in often to shmooze and slurp Popsicles), these framed, weathered renderings of the owner and their prominent position on the wall worked, despite Moshe's joking, to give the bright, closet-sized room a faintly melancholic air. The third and largest portrait there was a fading magazine photograph whose subject wore his thinning hair pomaded and his mustache bushy, like Moshe's, though there was also a trace of showiness, a slight pimpy ooze that tickled that familiar, defiant deadpan, and made me uncertain: Was this really Moshe? What was he doing with his picture in a magazine? And sure enough, when I asked if that was *him* in the photo up there, he gave me a funny look, then clicked his tongue and explained with his usual mixture of irritability and good humor that no, actually, it was "Connor," the actor in "that television movie." I wasn't sure who Connor was, but kept quiet as he sighed and continued, sounding suddenly more wistful, less interested in cheerful banter. "He is dead. We were friends."

His wife, too, had died several years before, and now he kept the place open till late at night, so that a few older men, some of them also widowers, would stop by to sit and keep him company. On Friday mornings, the newspaper stand filled with customers and the smells of the multicourse Sabbath dinner his grown daughters were cooking in the adjacent kitchen, and once he ordered me sternly to knock on his front door and ask for my newspaper if I ever came before Friday sundown and found the kiosk closed. I gave my word.

Sitting in front of his stand beneath a huge plastic parasol, Moshe saw most everyone who left his side of the neighborhood on foot and those who returned walking — familiar residents (old-timers or newcomers, sooner or later Moshe knew them all) as well as the dozens of Palestinian workers who hurried in cautious anonymity past his kiosk, en route, early morning, from the eastern to the western sides of the city and who straggled back home again in tired twos or threes around dark. Sometimes a furtive-looking Hasid would stray a few blocks over from Mea She'arim, the strictly centripetal ultra-Orthodox enclave, in search of a lottery ticket, cigarettes, or a peek at the secular headlines. On Sundays, the main pedestrian traffic would move in a north–south direction, as the Ethiopian priests in their black or burgundy cassocks, swirling magicians' capes, and color-coded tarbooshes would parade, accompanied by a gaggle of female pilgrims draped with white gauze shawls. They moved in loping, elegant clusters from the consulate and church complex on the Street of the Prophets to their Old City compound, an entire stuccoed village constructed on the roof of the Church of the Holy Sepulchre.

Though I don't know if Moshe registered the particulars of all those who came and went, in drabness and exotic color, throughout these long days, I always considered his stand an unofficial border crossing, and he himself a benevolent sort of guard: When I passed beyond his lookout point, I had entered the city-at-large, a place still familiar but never so intimate as the world of these few square blocks. Likewise, most nights when I made may way back from a movie, he would notice, tip his head toward me, and wave, and I would feel a great wash of relief at almost reaching home.

When I left, I was usually heading for a bus that would take me "to work" at a cineplex on the outskirts of town, or else I would walk toward the *shuk* — which both served as a tempting destination and an excuse to wander. It was with a ripple of pleasant surprise that, after years of these meandering shopping trips, I found Thoreau's etymology of *sauntering*. "Which word," he writes, "is beautifully derived 'from idle people who roved about the country in the Middle Ages, and asked charity, under pretense of going *à la Sainte Terre*,' to the Holy Land, till the children exclaimed 'There goes a *Sainte-Terrer*,' a Saunterer — a Holy-Lander." Here I was, then, long since arrived in the Holy Land, and still roving idly. . . . Though Thoreau himself, one imagines, wouldn't fare too well in modern Jerusalem. With his purist's sense of natural amazement he would no doubt be offended by (or perhaps allergic to) the sight of open weedy spaces alongside partly built hotels, or the perfect tissue-paper blooms of the apricot trees a few yards from the traffic's palpable stench — not to mention his curious declaration, later in that same essay, "Walking," that it is "too late to be studying Hebrew; it is more important to understand . . . the slang of today."

Downtown, too many cars and exhaust-spewing buses jockeyed for too little space. Since 1967, Jerusalem's municipal boundaries had swollen, for reasons both practical and political, and many businesses had fled to the low-rent suburbs, leaving a peculiar phenomenon to develop in the city's once-thriving nucleus: an overpopulated ghost town. In recent years many of the establishments along this main route had taken on a desperate, clearance-sale, everything-must-go air. Some of the older storefronts remained, their proprietors stooped, their signs and awnings grimy with the dregs of half a century's worth of passing diesel fuel. Two famous pharmacies fit into this category (though they did a better business than most and kept their windows scrubbed and their facades freshly painted), as well as several shabby appliance shops, jewelers, one grocery, and a few small, Central European–styled department stores, where the elderly female employees all wore scowls that seemed to come with their matching cotton uniforms, wigs, and ugly flat-soled shoes. But for the most part Jaffa Road had been colonized of late by a string of garish bargain clothing outlets, bridal shops, toiletry wholesalers, and international fast-food chains whose loudly familiar logos were especially offensive in these dilapidated surroundings. Into the graceful stone arcades had been shoved any number of ticky-tacky signboards announcing the latest business come to roost, and even occasional English directives to HAVE A GOOD TIME or JUST DO IT. Shops closed faster than they opened along this stretch (or opened–closed in a single breath: Sometimes they did both in the course of a few short, unprofitable months). Often, after one of the older merchants died and the mourning notice appeared across the locked door of the store bearing the same family name as the deceased, the place would sit empty for months, as a scar.

Whether I considered it consciously or not — and I could not, every time, without going mad — the saddest and in some ways the spookiest moment of this particular walk always came as I passed Zion Square, the ostensible city center, where a hostile-looking double shaft of a bank building (oddly reminiscent of the Ten Commandments' twin tablets, with all the words rubbed out) and various bedraggled groups of stoned teenagers, noisy tourists, and soldiers on slouching terrorist-watch now stood, the ground around them littered with cigarette butts and mangled bumper stickers from the last political demonstration or Hasidic revival campaign that had passed through, loudly blasting a theme song and strewing propaganda. In their place, a few decades before, had been a cinema, *the* cinema, the Zion Cinema. On a desolate plot purchased from the Greek Orthodox Church, a wood and tin hut of a theater was built in 1912 — its inner walls decorated in elaborate trompe l'oeil fashion by a painter friend of Israel Guth, the owner, himself a Lvov-born, Berlin-trained sculptor and teacher at Bezalel, the newly founded national arts and crafts school. Long wooden benches were constructed specially for the space, electricity converted by a dynamo, and a white sheet hung for a screen. In 1920, after the roof collapsed in a serious snowstorm, Guth began construction of a grand stone movie house on the same spot, and the Zion came to function as the city's primary theater almost nonstop until 1979, when it was demolished. That dumb skyscraper was then lowered into the very heart of town as both a grave reminder and an omen of worse things ahead. The empty space under the building now served as a convenient late-night latrine for all the surrounding pubs.

I liked knowing that the main city square took its name from a movie house, and not from the notorious Mount a short distance away, though now that its namesake had been destroyed, the term *Zion Square* seemed all the more rudely ironic, even macabre. I'd never seen the theater except in photos and in Jerusalem painter and printmaker Ivan Schwebel's elegiac Zion Square series, rendered when the theater was already moribund. The marquee and neighboring Kupulsky's café seem eerily alive in those etchings, their surfaces scratched on in an urgent-looking rush, as if getting them down on paper might somehow hold them there, on the street. A 1925 photograph shows a hill of gravel by the site and, atop it, a huddled group of city people with walking sticks and dusty shoes. The men stare or squint while the women, in sleek flapped hats and low-waisted dresses, smile at the camera. These slightly overdressed Jews are identified in a caption as the members of Golinkin's Opera Company, engaged to sing *La Traviata* at the Zion. At City Hall, I'd leafed through carbon copies of the theater's British Mandate–era tax and coal receipts and admired the Munch-inspired letterhead that Guth and his business partner used to lodge a legal complaint against another theater owner, M. Y. Mizrachi, whose extravagant, three-color promotional placards, they claimed, violated the regulation size and two-toned format agreed upon by the Organisation of Talkies in Palestine.

ZION HALL
Prop. I. GUTH & I. PEREZ

תיאטרון ציון
גיט י. פרז

سيون

سينما

Besides piles of contracts and correspondence from lawyers, distributors, and religious authorities (including an agreement by the theater owners not to screen films on the Jewish Sabbath), there were formal letters, typed on the official stationery of the Goverment of Palestine, District Commissioner's Offices, Jerusalem District, Jerusalem, signed by the Secretary of the Central Censorship Board, declaring, for example, "Gentlemen, I have the honour to refer to licence No. 1391 dated the 27th February, 1934, in respect of the film 'King Kong' which has been licensed in Palestine for *adults only*," and, later that same year, in the sterner mode of the unsmiling British civil servant who has, perhaps, spent a few too many years at this particular post, "Sir, My attention has been drawn to the fact that the licence in respect of the film 'ALLEZ OOP' shown at the Zion Cinema on Saturday evening the 17th August, was not projected on the screen before the exhibition of the film, in contravention of the regulation made (in Palestine Gazette No. 220 of 1.10.1928) under Section 11 of the Cinematograph Films Ordinance No. 27 of 1927. Such contravention is punishable in accordance with Section 8(3) of the same Ordinance by a fine not exceeding LP.5. I should be glad if an early explanation in this regard is furnished to this office at an early date. I am, Sir, Your obedient Servant."

The same file also contained several notes from the theater's employees, in Hebrew and in broken English, as this one, scrawled in childish longhand during the first week of July 1933: "I beg to inform that I won't be able to work this night, as I am not in a good Health and feeling very bad. I have been

instructed to lay in bed for 24 hours. Thanking you in anticipation I am your Trully." This, alongside urgent pre–World
War II communications from the Committee for the Boycott of
German Goods, informing Messrs. Guth and Perez in the
strongest terms that the exhibition of the films *Gruss und Kuss
Veronika* and *La Chanson de L'adieu* had not been authorized
by the Committee and was therefore "FORBIDDEN in all theaters throughout The Land." This ban, as well as others of
its kind, was attached with a rusted paper clip to a discreetly
apolitical-sounding inquiry, dated June 10, 1935, from one
C. Lutz, Chancellor of the Consulate of Switzerland for Palestine
and Transjordan, who noted that, in light of the "considerable
German speaking element among the moving picture public . . .
there exists in Palestine a certain demand for German speaking
films." Perhaps the management of the Zion Hall cinema
would consider screening German-language Swiss pictures?
"Switzerland, as you know, is blessed with rich scenic beauty, a
factor which contributes greatly to the beauty of films made on
Swiss territory," wrote Lutz. "Inasmuch as most of the moviegoing public are of the European mentality, European films
have no doubt a greater appeal to them than American prod-
ucts which are in so many instances untrue to actual life."

I also thumbed through yellowing copies of *The Palestine
Post* to see what was playing there on the night of, say, Saturday,
September 4, 1937. From the weekend paper the day before:

20th Century-Fox Presents
THREE GREAT STARS
Wallace Beery
Barbara Stanwyck
John Boles

In their greatest triumph!
United in danger, laughter, and love in

A MESSAGE TO GARCIA

Here is a picture you will find unforgettable

On SATURDAY, September 4, at the
"ZION HALL"
twice nightly: 7.15 — 9.20

Matinees at 3 P.M.
1. THE MAN WHO BROKE the BANK at MONTE CARLO
2. THE PRISONER OF SHARK ISLAND

and . . .

April 2, 1943, marked the THIRD WEEK of Walter Pidgeon and Maureen O'Hara in HOW GREEN WAS MY VALLEY, twice every night at 7:15 and 9:20. On Thursday December 28, 1950, the now–*Jerusalem Post* advertised LOOK FOR THE SILVER LINING at the Zion and on Saturday May 17, 1958, one could see there "The year's most exciting and sensational musical!" Elvis Presley, Lizabeth Scott, and Wendell Corey in LOVING YOU, in Technicolor and Vistavision.

And the Zion had not been the only theater nearby. Two blocks away on that same May night, the Orion (now a McDonald's) advertised "The Famous Singer Abd El Halim Hafez, in A Film Full of Love Songs: NOS BEAUX JOURS." Around the corner, at the Orna, Eddie Fisher and Debbie Reynolds, "Today's most popular entertainers," appeared in BUNDLE OF JOY, "a film full of songs, fun and laughter." Meanwhile, across the street, at the Ron (today, home to Blockbuster Video), "the lavish Viennese picture SISSI" was screened in "Glorious Agfacolour." Just a stroll from there, the Or Gil, the Arnon, and the Studio boasted, respectively, HANKA ("An exciting Yugoslav film! Including Kolo the international dancing group"), THE LADY TAKES A FLYER ("Israel premiere!"), and A WOMAN'S WORLD ("It's a great big wonderful Woman's World because men are in it"). Around the block, at the foot of Agrippas Street, the Eden featured, for the second week,

The Anguish, Passion and Struggle
in the career of

Vincent Van Gogh

portrayed by
Kirk Douglas

LUST FOR LIFE

And as a weird premonition of creationist things to come, the Edison — Mr. Mizrachi's elegant Art Deco picture palace that was at the time of its 1932 opening the most luxurious theater in town and stands empty at present, forced shut by the stern will of its ultra-Orthodox neighbors, its marquee unmarked, doorways stoppered with cement blocks to keep out would-be squatters — that night advertised, without the frivolous help of promotional slogans or even a mention of its stars:

(Was it a porn film? I find no mention of this picture in any of my movie books.)

Though a few hovel-like cinemas still functioned downtown when I began work as a film critic, they were already, then, on their way to extinction. There was the Orion, with its tiny, airless auditoriums and screens not much bigger than large TV sets. The deaf Russian crone who sold "refreshments" on the second floor there sat napping nightly beside her pile of old-looking candy. The popcorn machine was broken, or maybe it worked and no one bothered to switch it on anymore. Nearby, the Ron continued to command a certain faded grandeur, yet most often a slightly morbid depression would settle in as the cheerful parade of preshow ads started up and I'd find myself alone with my notebook in the five-hundred-seat hall.

Plenty bleak on their own terms, these few remaining downtown movie theaters also stood as tomblike monuments to the fast-fading memory of the thriving, café-and-intelligentsia-filled Jerusalem of an earlier era. The passing of this once-vibrant secular cultural center was clear not just from the sorry condition of the cinemas, but also from the piles of books I would sometimes find in the trash on my walks around town, presumably placed there after the death of yet another elderly bibliophile. At one time quite numerous in the city, the ranks of these hungry, general readers were dwindling rapidly, and one afternoon I discovered an entire library of handsome leather-bound and beautifully paper-wrapped volumes in Hebrew, German, English, Yiddish, and French, dumped by a stinking bin of garbage a few blocks from our house. Working as fast as we could — the sky seemed to darken more quickly that day — Peter and I and a few curious passersby (including the blond teenaged son of some American Christian missionaries who were quietly renting the apartment next door) crouched near the plastic bins, desperately pulling from between the smelly heaps of Pampers and banana peels any book that might possibly interest us or someone we knew. A few neighborhood children came to watch and giggle from a distance, and though I offered them several picture books I'd found, they looked so bewildered at the prospect of accepting the gift, I realized they had probably never owned a book and didn't understand the concept. Unfortunately, it was already well into dusk and I had no time to explain (around dawn the garbage trucks would come and haul the whole collection away).

At one point, several small, bearded, fedora-wearing men emerged from the synagogue nearby, in search of holy books, not to read, but to save from desecration. We pulled what we could for them from the mess and unearthed in the process one volume of Eliezer Ben Yehuda's massive dictionary, the first comprehensive lexicon of ancient and modern Hebrew, published painstakingly, one installment every few years, starting in 1910, by the Lithuanian-born scholar and fervent nationalist who saw the redemption and ingathering of his people as both a physical and linguistic challenge. According to legend, he refused to speak any language but Hebrew from the moment in 1881 when he stepped off the boat in Palestine (his wife had little choice but to follow verbal suit), and he immediately began collecting old words and coining new ones for his dictionary, so intent was he on saving the Hebrew language from the trash bin of history — to which his efforts had, on this particular afternoon, been most unceremoniously returned.

Our own rescue mission was related but hardly so grand or effective as his, and as we pushed through the piles, we looked for some sign of the missing sixteen volumes of his dictionary. But soon it grew too dark to read the words on the spines and the covers before us, so we gave up and had to make do with a single, deep red leather-and-suede-bound fragment, traced in gold, of Ben Yehuda's lifework, volume number thirteen, which begins with the verb *karar,* "to chill or to cool," and ends with the adjective *ratzui,* "beliebt; aimé; beloved."

⋊⋄⋄⋉

Two years after I took the job reviewing movies, the last down-town movie theater in Jerusalem closed its doors for good. While it was hard to feel much nostalgia for poorly heated places like the Ron and the Orion, with their ripped screens, lousy acoustics, and smell of antiseptic floor soap, the Zion was something else. Though I'd never seen the theater in person, I felt its symbolic loss profoundly, both every time I passed its former location and whenever I mounted the bus for that long ride out to the Mall — a synthetic American-styled void, built of Italian marble, by Canadian architects, over the remains of a Palestinian village. The demise of Malha, as it is still called, was more glaring than that of most emptied-out Arab towns only because the minaret of its mosque remained standing in the midst of the Israeli condominiums since constructed there. This lone spire loomed above the parking lot of the Mall, and as I traipsed across the asphalt from the bus stop, I had to work hard not to look up. "At the foot of the hill on which the vil-lage was built were a spring and a well," says one history book. "The immediate neighborhood of the village was bare, but there were vineyards to the east, and to its south grew olives and roses, as well as fig trees and various grain."

At other times, my moviegoing would take me to the city's industrial zone, built near the site of a fifties transit camp for new immigrants from North Africa. There, after dismounting the bus, a fifteen-minute walk awaited me, through a poorly tended housing project, where dirty little children and skittish street cats darted across my path, past a set of plasticky house-wares stores, then alongside a lot filled with purple thistles, broken bottles, and rusty, junked car hulls. Only then would I arrive at my destination, a faceless cement cineplex with a huge parking lot for a moat.

While I'd much rather have walked the five minutes from my front door to the Zion, or ten to the Edison, in the absence of these long-lost possibilities I half-enjoyed the boulder-strewn landscape around this particular structure, though I suspected it was populated by a few ghosts of its own. The road leading down to the theater was, on the whole, very quiet, yet its gaping, littered stasis lacked the calm of an open field. The emptiness there seemed recent, willed, as if something else — another Arab village? an ancient burial ground? — had once occupied this space. For all its silence, the air felt oddly charged. Now, aside from a few automotive-parts shacks and an abandoned snack bar, there was but a single house, a cubic stone structure with a tiled outdoor courtyard, a spacious doghouse, chicken-wire fence, and swirl of spidery pink bougainvillea. Just twice did I glimpse any sign of life there. One afternoon two pea-cocks appeared, magically strutting from around the back. They were gone when I passed just a few hours later, and I never saw them again.

Another time a small shrieking child burst from the gate and barreled before me, heading straight for the highway. Without thinking (I was already late for my movie, *Metro,* with Eddie Murphy), I began to scramble after him, and he darted away, scuttling toward the garbage-clogged weeds, into which I fol-lowed, trying to reason with him as I reached to grab his little striped shirt. The boy was tiny but quick and his lungs grew huge as he thundered for his father — who, it became clear, was nowhere nearby and had broken some promise to see him — his face turning the frightening shade of boiled beets as he fled. After a few minutes of my lame attempts to soothe the boy as I struggled to catch him, his mother finally emerged from the house, dull-eyed, wiry thin, and obviously exhausted by the child and what I imagined was a chase that had lasted several years. In sluggish slow motion she pursued him farther into the weeds, ignoring my presence and so freeing me to run off and sit in the dark.

NOT IN TWO THOUSAND YEARS

jacko ohana had two different wardrobes
and four different names, all for separate occasions. When he
stood behind the coolers at his fish stand in the *shuk,* he wore
a long, denim-blue smock spattered with carp blood and a vel-
veteen turquoise skullcap, traced with silver thread. These two
garments (the workaday gruesome and
the colorfully ornate) combined to give
him the look of a high priest preparing a
sacrifice at the Temple altar.

Then, after his retirement, on the days
when he would hold court opposite the
stand and greet old customers and
friends as his two grown sons, Chaim
and David, attended to the usual work
of stocking, cleaning, bagging, selling
the fish, and arguing bitterly with one
another, he appeared decked out in his
best pastel dandy-wear: pressed cotton
shirts in creamy sherbet shades, light
seersucker or khaki pants with tidy creases and cuffs, a trim
windbreaker, and his trademark open-toed orthopedic sandals
with clean purple or pale blue socks. "You're looking very nice
today," I would tell him. To which he would usually respond
with a combination of bashful pride and the troubling new

weariness that had crept into his voice since he'd stopped working and taken up the job, instead, of being a semi-invalid.

"I was at the hospital today for my treatment. It's only right I should show my respect for all the *professors*." He punctuated the final word with both a lilting French flourish and a tired shake of the head.

Jacko's cosmopolitan ability to balance at one and the same time several languages, deportments, and haberdashers was what first endeared him to me, though in truth I hadn't then fathomed the full range of his past: his middle-class, moderately religious, French-and-Arabic-speaking, Casablanca background didn't announce itself explicitly in the here-and-now but simply stamped the present tense of his demeanor with a mild grace, as much a product of his own personality as his mother tongue or the country of his birth. From the outset he seemed a decent man and responsible fishmonger, the most considerate and least aggressive or lecherous of the several I dealt with regularly at the *shuk*. And though I bought sardines or *bacalau*, trout or *rascasse* from him at least twice a week for several years, it was only later that I learned about his three other names, his father's Moroccan shoe factory, his eleven brothers and sisters, the childhood afternoons he spent on the docks of Casablanca, his two years on a Zionist collective farm in Tours, and how he arrived in Israel forty-five years ago at age twenty-one, miserably lonely and dejected.

I was masquerading, at the time, as a halfhearted sort of ethnographer and had decided to write a book about the *shuk* (an idea since abandoned). In preparation, I bought myself a compact tape recorder and spiral-bound notebook, which I would bring with me on my shopping trips and fill with flurried scribblings in a laughably hopeless attempt to capture the constantly changing sights, sounds, and scents all around me.

As I wrote, I also couldn't help feeling I was grossly altering the environment I sought to depict. Armed with paper and pen, I'd be assaulted by questions from all sides. Merchants, customers, even the illegally employed Palestinian boys, miniature scowling men who worked hauling boxes of fruit and garbage — everyone wondered what I was setting down in that notebook, such an oddity in this most oral of places. *Is it a love letter?* one tomato vendor asked me. *Still checking?* asked another man. *You're from Income Tax,* one announced, and several narrowed their eyes and accused me of working as an inspector for City Hall. Several times a particularly suspicious passerby would march right up and put his face between me and the paper, peering at the English chicken-scrawl there, as if to locate his own name and tear the page out (or maybe he would be flattered? I could never say for sure). The few times I admitted I was writing "a book" about the *shuk,* I was treated to a set of elaborately preprogrammed declarations about the heroic life of a *shuk* merchant who, much like the mythic American mailman, delivers the letters — or cucumbers, eggplants, bunches of dill — come rain or come shine, day in, day out. And with much false modesty. *We work hard, very hard. In the cold and the heat. It's our job. But we don't complain, here on the front lines.* This response, it bears saying, doesn't necessarily reflect the true feelings of the merchants so much as it does the down-home spiel they imagine a writer wants to hear, and the rote nature of the local-color stories they had come to expect from the newspapers, especially around election time, when the sentiments of a Mahaneh Yehudah pickle salesman were said to be a perfect indicator of how "the folk" would vote. Of course, if I pushed a little harder, I might be treated to the bilious flipside of this rosy picture: *The shuk disgusts me,* declared one vendor with a wilted inventory. *My dream is to get the hell out of this shithole.* Another paunchy middle-aged man announced himself proudly the mob boss of the market: *I keep no records! I pay no taxes! The authorities are terrified of me!* he declared a little too loudly to be true while his son, with one glass eye, bellowed into a cell phone that he'd just been pickpocketed on the bus. The man proceeded to lean across the heap of watermelons he was selling and spell his name, grabbing the notebook out of my hands to look and make sure I'd gotten it right.

Jacko was different. He seemed eager — even relieved — to find someone curious about his background, and the twenty years he had spent selling fish in the *shuk*. His own sons, for their part, couldn't have cared less. When they weren't screaming at each other, they would curse their father at the top of their lungs. Then Jacko would mutter his purse-lipped invective and I would turn my eyes away: I felt for both the gray-haired little man and his grown boys, who each had his own wife and children to support and who wanted nothing more than to be his own boss. (The shorter, older brother, Chaim, in particular, was sympathetic, in a taciturn way.) But neither my well-intentioned empathy nor anyone else's could help in the slightest to soften the painful public spectacle that took place as they thundered and fumed at one another, framed by the proscenium door of the fish stall. Several times, I arrived on the scene prepared to ask Jacko if he wouldn't mind sitting and describing for me how he had first come to work in the *shuk* . . . yet before I even drew close to the stand, their bellows filled the covered alleyway and made me wince. I never knew the precise subject they were wrangling about. It often seemed technical and petty, the quantity of St. Peter's fish and gray mullet ordered an excuse to let rip their darkest, most primal complaints. And although they made no attempt whatsoever to hide the intense hostility of their noisy arguments, I would slink away on these days, preferring to speak to father and sons when all were in a better mood, which is to say: separately. I had no desire to take sides or find myself caught in between.

But eventually I managed to eke out my request and Jacko didn't even blink before ordering me gently — *Come on Sunday, at eleven o'clock* — in a smooth, contented tone worlds away from the raw one he used with his sons. *Then we'll talk.* Although Jacko always sounded a bit hoarse, the slight pinch in his larynx periodically threatening to rob him of speech altogether, I was amazed at his cool command of several registers. The way he would shift in the course of a few seconds from an angrily bleated whisper for his children to a vigorous, clarion greeting for an old customer or friend seemed, like so much about him, a product of both willful dignity and an unconscious, almost naive frustration that his sons and his business were now for the most part out of his control. Jacko did not seem bitter. Most times, in fact, he stood his small square of ground with remarkable poise and humor. But when he was tired or when his sons were especially outspoken in their contempt for his cautious, Old World manners, his quiet perplexity took shape as a stunted sort of rage. I think they saw him as unmanly, a useless antique — and in some horrible sense he contributed to this caricature, and learned to play the part. Then his voice dwindled to a gnarled rasp and his body seemed to shrink. His shoulders lifted tight at his ears, his chin sunken to his chest, his gaze averted, he would play the role of wizened victim, frail and distracted as he shuffled and mumbled to himself.

Just as speedily, though, on the days when Chaim drove to the coast to buy fresh fish and the lazier, cross-eyed son, David (or Dudu, as he unfortunately preferred to be called), slept late and left the pudgy Palestinian teenager who worked as an assistant to open the shop, Jacko would spring into action and take up his vital old posture behind the counter, glinting fish cleaver in hand, suddenly restored to his former health and pluck. As I came to understand, his anger toward his children at once burdened him and egged him on, and he used these radical changes in his physical bearing and tone of voice as a flamboyant way of punishing them, showing them just how much they had hurt him. *What is THAT?* (He'd wait till they were near enough to hear his scornful words but would rarely address them head-on.) *Leaving* the worker *to open up? These children, they don't know what it MEANS to WORK. They think everyone OWES them.* Although I didn't doubt for an instant the genuine anguish the sons and father had caused one another over the years, Jacko's hyperbolic flipflops of tone and appearance occasionally bordered on the absurd. Once, for instance, as I approached the stand, I saw how his skin had loosened around the cheeks and jowls and taken on a grayish, unshaven hue. Edging toward the counter to say my tentative hello, I was sure that Jacko was dying right before my eyes of some hideous wasting disease. But when I asked him gingerly how he felt, he gave me a broad wink and explained in a playful stage whisper that he was fine except that he had gone to the doctor for a checkup and left his dentures there; they'd been thrown away by accident and now he was waiting for a new set. Hence his ghoulish demeanor, which he seemed happy to parade in front of his children, as a further sort of lashing, as if to say: *You* have made me old. *I can't eat!* He complained loudly. *I CAN'T CHEW!*

And now, when I asked Jacko if we might sit and talk, he used his tightened vocal chords in a different, calculated way. Even though we were alone at the fish stand, whiny reed music playing from a nearby radio, he answered my request in a hushed, conspiratorial tone. Would I like to visit his house? It might be quieter there. Did I know which bus to take to Mevasseret, the suburb where he lived? Could I find the place on my own?

At first I stood there, momentarily dumbstruck by his immediate enthusiastic answer and the series of questions he'd posed

— which seemed almost comical in response to *my* request to ask *him* questions. And before I even had time to think, he flashed me a big lady-killing grin and assured me that I shouldn't worry, I would be safe. His wife would be there too. "Of course," I stammered . . . eleven o'clock sounded fine. . . .

"Be healthy," he dismissed me with a brisk blessing. "All the best. Feel fine. I'll see you Sunday, God willing."

✕✿✿✕

"I studied, studied . . . *really STUD-IED* — and not just any old studies . . . First . . . I studied Torah, *how I studied!*" Jacko insisted, his one-man call-and-response style gaining momentum as he went on, his voice pitched solidly now in the depths of his chest, and now at the top of his head, the syllables stretched or shortened as the body of an accordion, to shade a word's meaning. "And then . . . *then* came the time, my father decided to register me in a regular school, a French school, *l'Alliance* . . . For this, people slept two nights on line." In staccato: *"Two-whole-nights-on-line."* And more gradually again, low, from the sternum: "It wasn't like *here,* where school is required, an *obligation.* What's that, an *obligation?* WE are obliged, WE should be grateful to study, to learn. GRATE-ful!" In the course of one sentence, he would alternate between baritone and falsetto, pianissimo and forte. Though the sound of Jacko's monologue was distinctly musical, it was the intricate dynamics and syncopation of his speech, not a simple melody, that gave it the quality of song. His talk was soft but percussive, modulating from sentence to sentence as an Andalusian orchestra does, speeding, slowing, then accelerating again as it moves through the proscribed rhythmic phases.

"All in all there was . . . one class: room for thirty-five, forty students. But *two hundred children* were waiting in line. . . . *Two HUN-dred CHILD-ren!* What can you do? There were

119

other schools, around the city — we'd have to be split up. So. So they sat us down, they tested us. My turn came and they asked me questions. Then . . . *then* they said to my father, Sir, where did this boy study? *Where? WHERE?* So he answered: He studied Torah. If he studied *Torah,* they said to my father, he'll have no problems. *NO PROBLEMS,* nothing will be a problem for him if he studied Torah. *No-thing* . . . So they sent me to a Christian school, a school just for Christians, *La Flamme Blanche,* very high level, a school for foreigners. . . . We didn't agree at first, but they said: *On-*ly a place like this is right for you. What will you do there, at that *other* school? You know many things, *many things* that they don't yet know in that class . . . what will *you* do *there? WHAT?*"

As he spoke of being seven years old, Jacko pulled plastic soda bottles from the refrigerator and arrayed them on the spotless counter. There were at least eight different kinds of soft drink, the totality of which he offered up with a distracted shrug, interrupting his almost-sixty-year-old reminiscences to ask me if I preferred regular or diet. With ice or without? Was I hungry?

"During the *war*" — he lingered over the word, pausing to pull a plastic container from the freezer and empty the contents into a saucepan — "they got us ready for the Germans, taught us German and things. They didn't know I was Jewish. I was the only one, but *they* didn't know, we didn't stress it, see. *What for?* They taught us to walk, walk like soldiers, they taught us German songs. At four o'clock, when school was over, we'd go down to the cafeteria and march, *back* and forth and *back* and forth, like little soldiers, *back* and forth . . . I told my father and my father, he listened, and then he said *enough. ENOUGH.* He took me out of that school and put me in another school. In the end, everything was fine. It all worked out. No problems. Do you like hot peppers?"

Aside from a mute canary that sat in a cage in the middle of the large living room ("A neighbor's cat snuck in here last week and scared the bird," claimed Jacko, without irony; "now she's too frightened to sing"), we were alone in the cool, cavernous house. His wife, he explained, had been called off to help a sick aunt at the last minute . . . he hoped I wouldn't mind. "Not to worry, I'm harmless," he winked and then immediately emitted a protracted geriatric sigh and shuffled off to pull plates and forks from the tidy piles his wife kept in her glass-fronted cabinets.

We had traveled together on the bus from the *shuk*. Jacko insisted he pay for my ticket, and we wound out of town, onto the curved highway bound for Tel Aviv and around the once-barren, now-overpopulated slopes that marked the entrance to the city, the valleys still cut through with green. Then as we arrived at this peculiar, hilly suburb, the driver downshifted and the bus lurched into its overweight mode, heaving and puffing up and up past dozens of pale, new or half-finished "villas," drooping palm trees, and bulbous aloe plants. When we got off the bus there was no sound save the steady, distant whoosh of trucks on the road below and an occasional cricket chirp. In the street, we met an acquaintance of Jacko's, a flirtatious little Moroccan grandma. Jacko bowed slightly and the woman gig-gled, then demanded to know who I was. "A *client* of ours." He introduced me with a friendly sort of formality. "She is writing a report on the *shuk* and I am helping her. I have offered to help her with her report."

"Why not?" The wrinkled slip of a coquette laughed again then squeezed my hand with surprising force and ordered Jacko to give me something to drink. "She'll dry up, Zakie. Poor thing, let her drink!"

This was, it turned out, the diminutive by which his wife and older friends called him, and of all the monikers that applied to Jacko Ohana — *"Isaac Zakie Jaques,"* as he transcribed his

names for me in the loopy Latin letters of a diligent schoolboy
— it always struck me as the best suited to his personality, or at
least to his spryer and less self-pitying side. The slight French
zip of the Z and the youthful *ie* both fit his dashing manner. His
wife, Rachel, turned out to be a pretty, round-hipped redhead,
far too vivacious and girlish-looking to be a grandmother
twelve times over, though she was. When she called his name,
Za-kie, she sang it out across a harmonic interval and sounded
like she was tickling him. The way she affixed his name to every
sentence seemed part of an intimate understanding between the
two of them, a means of taking the bite off the constant orders
she issued: *Zakie, open the blinds. Reach me that plate, Zakie.*
Others referred to him as "Zakie" as well but they were all elderly and Moroccan and appeared to have known him since he
was young enough to have earned such a bouncy name. For me
to do so seemed almost rude, assuming too close or disrespect-
ful a bond. I continued to address him as Jacko, also a nick-
name but somehow more neutral.

"*How I studied!*" he resumed the refrain. "I would finish
school at four, I'd go to the yeshiva to study Torah, many
things, all kinds of things, *important* things. Afterward, I'd go
to another place, a club, Na'im Zemirot, do you know what
that is, Na'im Zemirot? What a place, *what . . . a . . . place . . .*
We'd learn songs and prayers there, how to pray in synagogue,
we learned things, *ma-ny* things, many many good things . . .*"
Jacko trailed off, his tone grown foggy and limply nostalgic as
it sometimes would when I hadn't asked a precise enough question: Describe the house you grew up in. Or: Where did you
spend your first night in Israel? Have you heard of the town
Ocaña in Spain? I wondered if *Ohana* came from Ocaña, if his
ancestors had once lived there. This suggestion on my part, of
a family tree whose roots stretched back more than five hundred years across the Mediterranean, to Morocco, over the

Straits of Gibraltar, and inland, back toward a pre-Inquisition Spanish village not far from Toledo, was met with a confused squint from my host. He had an uncle once, he said, his mother's brother, who vacationed in Spain. . . . No, he'd never heard of Ocaña.

"Did you — like it, all that studying?" I asked rather thickly as Jacko continued to putter in the kitchen. Again he shrugged and pulled two white rolls from a plastic bag.

"Pah. What's that, *like it?* I had no choice. That's the custom, that's the practice, and that's the way it's done." This last proclamation emerged from his lips as a single, memorized *rat-a-tat-tat,* one I imagined he'd heard many times as a boy and had wielded against his own children when they were younger and had whined about some religious rule or early-bedtime order. "Like it or not. No one ever even asked me, Do you like it? *Did I like it?* That's the practice. Nothing to be done. If you want to learn you have to study. *WORK!* That's that. That's life." I nodded, feeling a bit literal and American as Jacko brought forth our lunch: rich fish fritters stewed in spicy tomatoes, along with four or five bowls of colorful fried peppers and olives, cracked green and shriveled black. He began to eat by pulling off a piece of roll and dipping it into the sauce. I found myself doing the same.

"When I was young, we wanted to build ourselves a club. We had no money. Our organization, the Zionist Youth, I was in the Zionist Youth — we wanted to build a club, for the members. A club. So we brought two Arabs, professionals, and we worked with them. They knew the profession and we worked with them, we learned to do hard work: We *dug,* we *built,* we *worked,* worked hard there. *HARD!* After that, we went to France for training, we were trained in Tours. . . . There's a city, Tours. Do you know it? Where is it?" He stopped chewing to check my answer.

"In the Loire . . ."

"That's correct. *Dans l'Indre-et-Loire*. Right right right. So near Tours there are towns, *villagim*" — he used the French word with a plural Hebrew suffix — "agricultural *villages*. So they sent us to one *village*, a little *village* called Runi, and there was a — how do you it say in Hebrew — a *ferme, une ferme. Qu'est-ce que c'est, une ferme?*"

"Yes, *une ferme* . . . a farm," I answered in English, my Hebrew also momentarily gone.

"Like, like what Arik Sharon has . . . they say he has *une ferme* — a farm, *chavah*." He found the Hebrew word. "That's it, a *chavah*, a farm. . . . So they took us there and they taught us things, many things, about agriculture and all. *Cows. Chickens. Tractors.* We were there for two, almost three years. I learned all kinds of things. . . .

"Then we came here, after two years. From Marseilles. They sent us to a kibbutz . . . ach, the first day I could already see already I couldn't handle it. I'm used to *business*" — and here he chose the English word. "To work like that, you know. Kibbutz, it's not for me. I'm urban, a city boy. My father owned a shoe factory. My grandfather was the head of the union, the shoemakers' union. They would come to him, the workers, with their complaints, for him to decide. Like a *judge* he was, they listened to him, his word was like law. An important man! Now, Casablanca . . . Casablanca was something wild — *something* wild! — Where are you from?" Again he stopped and turned the question back at me.

"From the United States."

"From the United States." He sounded doubtful, or maybe a bit disappointed. "So how do you know French?"

"From school, you know —"

"Ah, I see, you studied French in school." He paused for a minute over his fish, and seemed for a minute to be very far away, caught somewhere between Tours and Marseilles, Casablanca and Mevasseret. Then, just as quickly, he returned to his thought, without waiting for a question. "You know my father, may his memory be blessed, he always thought that I'd do something big, some-*thing,* some-*thing BIG* with my life. That I'd be at least a lawyer. He thought there should be at least one lawyer in the family. . . ."

Jacko never finished his sentence. He looked flushed and intent for an instant — filled briefly, perhaps, with the need to make a declaration, to give some official accounting of how it was that his father's promising little boy, the lawyer-to-be, had come to spend the past half century as a manual laborer. (Before he opened his fish stand, he explained, he had built roads, been a dock worker, and packed eggs for Tnuva, the government agricultural cooperative.) Instead he turned his eyes to his plate and switched in a determined, upbeat tone to a list of brothers and sisters, eleven all told. He was the fifth child. One brother was a dentist. Another brother was a dentist. One had to have open-heart surgery. Two still lived in Morocco. Some were in France — he had visited there last year, it was just a week, not long enough — and a few others lived in the south of Israel, in Dimona.

He seemed eager to recount certain stories he had already rehearsed — about the ordeal of leaving Morocco, for instance, and the three times he'd bid his whole family good-bye then boarded the train filled with happy Jews singing Hebrew songs, made the long trip to the Algerian border only to be turned back, and back again, and one more time before finally crossing over. "All for *l'idéalisme,*" as he put it, a little wistfully. I could sense almost instantly when he was resorting to a well-worn anecdote and when he was pushing to think his way through a particular response, as when he admitted the other half of this picture-book, Zionistic story ("it was a lot of propaganda"), and confessed that he'd been miserable at first, a young man alone in a strange place. He had even decided to leave, and had booked his passage back to Casablanca, but then had another change of heart, standing on the dock at Haifa, and convinced himself to try and stick it out a little longer — not because of *l'idéalisme* but because he was afraid. His mother, by then a widow, had written to warn him that the situation in Morocco had taken a turn for the worse. She could not be responsible for what might happen if he returned. (She sent him newspaper clippings to make sure he saw that what she said was true, and not just maternal fretting.) The Jews were no longer wanted there, after the French had gone, and Casablanca was a different place, dirty, chaotic . . . I let him talk on, rarely interrupting or asking him to finish a labyrinthine tale that he'd abandoned in the middle or rounded off with a truism — *That's the way it is . . . Nothing to be done . . . Everything will be all right.* Following out the beginning-middle-end of his various stories seemed secondary to the immediate fact of his posture in the present, his echoing cadences, and the unaware but elegant way he zigzagged between decades and continents. I was also amazed by his almost breathless readiness to recount for me, a mere acquaintance, all these far-off pieces of his past. Most of these memories seemed to have been corked up inside him for a very long time, and now they crowded each other, demanding to be let out, to spill. Although I'd intended to ask about the *shuk* and the years Jacko spent selling fish there, we barely touched on the subject: The rest of these remembered details seemed far more urgent in the telling, while the particulars of how he'd passed the last two decades were reduced in this free-associative version of his biography to no more than an afterthought.

Laughing, he told the story of how he worked as a teenager at an American military base in Casablanca "As a chef! *A certified chef!* And what does that mean? There was an American

there, in charge. He was my friend, Mister Max Bund. A Jew!
He said to me" — and here he tried out a few words of muddy
English — "*Zakie,* he said, I geev you a certificate, *un certificat
professionnel,* you work in ze kitchen, yes? *But I can't cook!* I
said. *Forget this!* says Max Bund. He was right! I didn't *need*
to, you see. . . . For eight hours a day I poured juice from cardboard boxes, into a big tank. . . . Every day the same thing,
every day the same juice!"

Max Bund figured in another tale, too, about a date Jacko
made to take "his girl" to the beach for the day.

"Your wife?"

"This was years before my wife!" he smiled crookedly. But
he had no money and so he challenged Max Bund to a game of
7-11. "I rolled seven-eleven, seven-eleven . . . I cleaned him out!
What a game!"

And then (would I like some more fish? Another glass of
soda?) he told of the afternoons he'd sometimes spend as a boy
on the docks of Casablanca ("we couldn't study *all* the time"),
watching the ships sail in with nets and nets of the freshest fish,
"every kind of fish you can imagine. Any fish you could want."
The *shuk* there, he said, was nothing like the *shuk* here. "It was,
how do you say, civilized, organized, so *beautiful.*" The fixed
prices were listed on a huge blackboard at the entry gates, and
a porter would follow you and haul your purchases — all the
way back home! They locked those gates at night, heavy iron
gates, with fancy colored metalwork. "I don't believe, *I do not
believe* that in two *thousand* years — two thousand years —
we'll ever come close to the kind of order that they had there. *I
don't believe it!*"

Then there was the time, around Jacko's bar mitzvah, when
his father was sick, paralyzed, "almost *dead,*" but was cured by
Dr. Ben Zakane, "a ve-ry, ve-ry important man, his son married
my sister. He was minister of health in Morocco, in *those* days."

The doctor's cure? "STOP DRINKING It is FORBIDDEN to drink alcohol. . . . But then my father, may his memory be blessed, he got it into his head that he wanted to go to a holy man's grave, to make a pilgrimage to the grave of Avraham, Master of the Miracle, in the village of Azzemour. So we went, I went with him, we were on our way to pray when he heard shouting, singing, laughing. *What happened?* we asked. They told us: *There was a woman, crawling on all fours — and she walked! On her feet! Eight days she sat beside the grave — without food, without water, without anything. And after eight days, she stood and she walked.* People were happy! Singing, celebrating, drinking arak, cognac, passing the bottle for a toast, *l'chaim!* So what could my father do? He said he *had* to drink, that's the way it's done: *The holy man will do what he wants. If he wants to kill me, so I'll die. Faith!* And he drank, and then he drank some more and more and SURE ENOUGH — he was sick again, and my mother was angry at me, she said WHAT *IS* THIS? *How could you let him drink?* Dr. Ben Zakane was mad too, an important man, he didn't have time to waste on a patient who wouldn't listen. He told us, *There is NO cure for stubbornness!*

"I am sick too, you know, not a healthy man . . ." he wiggled down into his chair and lowered his voice for effect. "It's my children, you see, *they make me ill, REALLY.*" And just as suddenly as he'd slouched over, he sprung up and opened a kitchen cabinet, from which he pulled a hefty black briefcase. "AND *THIS*" — he gestured like a magician as he snapped open the latch — "is my emergency medical kit."

He showed off the electronic heart monitor with its automatic ambulance-summons button and tangle of colored wires. "Red goes on the left," he explained, a wicked gleam in his eye. "Do you know how I remember *that?*" He placed the little suction on his breast pocket and grinned. "*Red* — for communists — *on the left!* Do you see?"

We chuckled at his joke and I said that I had probably better be going. He had been very generous but now he was tired, and maybe we should continue this some other time — "Wait!" Jacko looked startled and a bit sad, as if he couldn't bear to be left alone. Would I like to see the house first, before I left? He would give me the grand tour.

After he demonstrated the electric blinds behind the dining room table, he showed off the picture window in the living room, that faced onto "a real American lawn." This modest patch of green, bordered with purple petunias, was his reason for living here, he said, outside of the city and away from the crowded neighborhoods where he'd raised his children. One of these neighborhoods turned out to be our own: He and his family had lived for more than fifteen years just around the corner from what was now our apartment, in the public housing project where we had visited Meir and Yaffa, something I hadn't known before but which seemed, when I heard it, to account in part for the instinctive affection I'd felt toward Jacko when I first met him. That he had spent so many years surrounded by our neighbors in this landscape made him a sort of neighbor-once-removed. (As it happened, he had also worked for years at the Tnuva warehouse, a building now converted to the airless headquarters of the newspaper for which I worked. Jacko explained in his thoughtful singsong that the eggs were once packed where the printing presses are today, the fish took up the editorial offices, and the chicken coops filled the news-room.) He wasn't sorry they'd left the city. "I've had enough of the *noise,* the *tiny rooms.* I'm too old for that now, it's time to relax a little, stretch my legs out."

Up a carpeted flight of stairs, the master bedroom looked across a ridge at the sprawling municipal cemetery, several steep hillsides packed tight with pale, blocky gravestones, an entire neighborhood populated by the new city's Jewish dead.

The opposite wall was covered with ceiling-to-floor closets, which Jacko flung open to reveal no less than twenty neatly pressed men's suits, hanging in a row. "If I lived *abroad*," he said, in a proud but factual way, "I'd dress up every day."

He led me into a small side room, with a TV set, a sofa, and another freestanding closet, which contained, it turned out, dozens and dozens of men's cotton shirts, a full Jay Gatsby array in Jacko's favorite shades — pink, light yellow, powder blue, cream, lavender, pistachio green — alongside a hanger of immaculate silk ties. He fingered the cuffs of one peach shirt and smiled faintly. "I could dress so nicely . . . if I didn't work, you know, with the fish it's so messy."

"You *do* look nice, though —" I started to protest, but Jacko waved his hand through the air as if to brush my silly words away.

"That's *nothing*," he insisted, his voice now more distant. "But that's how it is. That's life."

THE LAND AFAR OFF

we had now lived together in jerusalem
for more than five years. While that period elsewhere might
have sped by in a noncommittal flash, here its passing carried
a certain fateful weight. In relation to our friends who had
spent most if not all of their years in the city, of course, it still
made us greenhorns — me especially,
since Peter had put down roots earlier,
in a different (closer, simpler, quieter,
greener) Jerusalem, one that had since
been buried and paved over but had
been described to me at great, wistful,
and occasionally irritating length. *This*
Jerusalem, right now, was the only one I
would ever know, after all, and hearing
about the charmed days of yore, when
fresh chickens were subsidized and
open, poppy-covered fields abounded,
would only make me rueful. Still, the
city had clearly become our home, with

all the comfort and annoyance, the love and disgust that the
term implies.

At the same time, there was something about this particular
place — its smallness, perhaps, or the constant engagement it
demanded — that necessitated periodic escape, a change in

emotional air pressure. Going away was also a means of gaining perspective: To depart and return was to have one's old enthusiasms at least partially restored. This process worked in mysterious ways, since (as both my own experience and several thousand years of fraught Middle Eastern history make clear) leaving Jerusalem was not like leaving any other place. Often, in turning one's back and going away from it, one felt oneself drawn nearer — just as, when caught up in its messy push-and-pull, one frequently longed to be elsewhere. Yet this perverse nostalgia for the city left behind was not mere sentimentality: There was an uncanny aspect to it as well. No matter where one wandered, one was always, somehow, orbiting Jerusalem, spinning out from its intricate force field.

One year, in midwinter, we left by bus and traveled north to the once-Roman, now-podunk town of Beit She'an, on the Jordanian border.

Then, after a taxi ride that lasted long enough for the driver to scowl and assure us that the other country so close by was "a waste of time, there's nothing to see there," we passed over the border. The newfangled crossing was eerie, an enormous, well-appointed complex, designed to accommodate the hordes of eager tourists some wishful government official had apparently anticipated would be pushing and shoving to make their way over into the New Middle East. But it hadn't happened and, with the exception of a score of bored-looking girl soldiers, noisily cracking their chewing gum as they stamped our passports, visas, and exit-tax receipts in triplicate, we were alone. After another bizarrely disproportionate passage — half a minute's inching bus ride over the few feet of bridge erected to mark the legendary River Jordan, at this spot no more than a trickle — we were welcomed to the Royal Hashemite Kingdom by a staggered series of billboard portraits of King Hussein, looking dapper with his red kaffiyeh and trim mustache. We were also greeted by several straight-backed, chain-smoking Jordanian soldiers, all mustachioed as well, and decked out in far neater uniforms — blue and starched, with Arabic numbers emblazoned across the breast pockets — than the Israelis, who wore olive green and kept their collars unbuttoned, their hair uncombed, silver rings on their fingers.

We had both needed to get as far from the grind and exhaust of Jerusalem as possible, but it was only now that we'd crossed the border and found ourselves standing on the other side — facing out across a ragged plane of banana trees and marsh weeds, no other humans in sight — that we realized how far we had come, even after such a short journey. Most Jewish tourists from Israel drive south and ride over in air-conditioned buses to take in the famous views at Petra, a place we also wanted, at some point, to see. For now, our goal was more one of departure than of arrival: To *leave* our apartment, street, neighborhood, city, country — this was the idea. Where we would *come to* was another matter altogether. In a fairly random way, we'd chosen as our first destination a hill town called Ajlun. There was, we read in the guidebook, a fortress in Ajlun that had been built in the twelfth century by a nephew of Saladin, to repel the Crusaders. It had been damaged by the Mongols, rebuilt by the Mamluks, used as a garrison during Ottoman times, hit hard by earthquakes in the last two hundred years, and then partly restored for touristic purposes. Its mountainous obscurity sounded like a good antidote to our own notorious city on a hill.

Now we had to get there, a prospect that suddenly seemed at once exciting and a bit scary for all its unknown logistical particulars. Peter had been studying Arabic and could function well in his controlled YMCA-classroom setting, but this would be his first extended, real-life linguistic test. I vowed to keep silent and let him speak as we walked to the end of the long, flat road that led away from the border, and approached one of the taxi drivers waiting there. Peter cleared his throat, tried a few words, and the man responded casually, flicking his cigarette ash as he spoke. To our amazement, the Arabic seemed to work. We were off. The radio blared tinny Eastern pop and we rolled down the rickety windows to let the cool breeze blast us and clear our crowded heads. This air turned brisker and colder the higher we traveled, past flocks of goats and uniformed schoolchildren who would scatter from their respective paths in the middle of the dusty road as the cab sped toward them, alongside empty fields, mosques, body shops, clusters of simple concrete or stone houses and vegetable stands, their signs painted in gaudy carnival shades . . . and into the hills around Ajlun, whose dark fortress we could see looming on a far-off ridge long before the road wound close and its name appeared on the road signs.

By late afternoon, we had arrived at the foot of the jagged castle. After taking a room that faced the structure, we climbed to the roof of the roughly hewn fortress with its grassy moat and knots of boulder-strewn passages. How had the soldiers here managed to keep from freezing? The December chill outside took on an even icier edge inside the bleak halls. From the highest turret, we looked across in the direction of once-Crusader Jerusalem — whose actual shape was obscured in the haze and seemed from here no more than a distant memory, abstract on the horizon. We stood watching as this western nonview (home?) faded into darkness and disappeared completely. Then, in the last remaining light around us, we descended the rocky stairs and began to walk downhill toward our capacious yet empty six-story hotel. We were alone but kept our voices hushed as we spoke into the blackness. There were no streetlights and none of the usual mild nature sounds I associate with the boondocks: crickets, frogs, the *hoo* of an owl. The air hung still and quiet, until we heard faint music pulsating from a building below that a large wooden sign declared to be a rest house. We decided to go in and warm ourselves there, and the place turned out also to be a kind of fortress, filled with serious waiters decked out in clean white shirts and black bow ties, waiting to serve . . . who? There were no other tourists in Ajlun, as far as I could see, aside from the middle-aged Jordanian couple we had seen coming out of the castle, she in high heels, he in a soft, double-breasted suit. Meanwhile, this rest house was set up, like the border and hotel, as if prepared to accommodate dozens of busloads of visitors, the tables each set with carefully folded cloth napkins, crystal, vases of plastic flowers. We ordered coffee, and it came, thick and sweet, in espresso-styled cups with saucers, alongside a large bottle of mineral water. As if to humor us, the maître d' ordered one of the waiters to flip off the local radio station they had been listening to and, after a few minutes, Whitney Houston's voice blared from the speakers. So we shivered in the barnlike restaurant to the sounds of American pop-soul, as four or five waiters stood at attention, watching our every move. We drank as slowly as possible, then ventured outside again, back into the colder cold, only to hear within four steps of the door the music swerve back to a native key. Who were they waiting for, I wonder?

Ajlun in the morning was a different place — crowded, bright, and bustling. The enigmas of the night before seemed to have evaporated with the predawn dew, and now the streets leading downhill from the fortress and our hotel were lively with young men hurrying to work, older men sitting and smoking outdoors on low straw stools, and women of all ages — most in slacks, pumps, and white head scarves — dragging little children and plastic grocery bags behind them. It was still early, not yet seven-thirty, and already the sandy cul-de-sac of a bus station had launched into full midday swing when we mounted a taxi-van bound southeast and found ourselves squeezed five to a seat, a radio talk show blaring, the air heavy with the scent of slightly medicinal cologne, pungent male sweat, and more of that ubiquitous unfiltered cigarette smoke.

We spent a full day wandering the sprawling Roman metropolis at Jerash, and as we moved between the staggered pillars and steep temple steps, the modern country where we lived both slipped farther and farther from sight and came more starkly into focus as just the latest in a parade of civilizations that had passed through the region like so many cars of a long circus train. I would sometimes get a similar fleeting feeling as I made my way through the alleys of Jerusalem's own Old City — though, not surprisingly, perspective (or the sudden vertiginous awareness of one's own historical negligibility) was harder to come by amid the familiar trappings of home. One had, really, to stand back in order to grasp it fully, which is precisely what happened as we made our way down ancient Jerash's abandoned stage set of a main drag, a lengthy stone street lined with a colonnade and worn into smoothed grooves by long-gone chariot wheels. No sooner had I begun to contemplate quite seriously my own ephemerality than this awareness turned to farce: We rounded a corner near the sunken cove of a Nymphaeum and almost tripped over a tangled pile of electrical wires and lighting equipment. This anachronistic heap was overseen with suntanned nonchalance by a few unmistakably Israeli film technicians. The members of this crew were taking turns heaving fake frescoes and Styrofoam rocks from a large truck whose Hebrew letters had been tactfully covered over, in preparation for a nighttime shoot of *Mortal Kombat II,* an American action movie sequel based on a video game. (So much for my desire to forget about my job for a couple of uncinematic hours.) It was not, though, just the Israelis who were engaged in the manufacture of spanking-new relics: Earlier in our wanderings we'd mounted a scruffy hill overlooking the town and come across a lone tent, from which came the dull clinking sound of a mallet striking metal. As we approached, a grinning local teenager sprang from between the flaps, eager to sell us a whole handful of freshly minted "Roman" coins, "guaranteed very old."

Later, toward evening, we reached Amman, a functional, modern city that seemed familiar in many ways. The gradual roll of the hills and the pale shades of the squarish modern buildings were a dingy, modest mirror image of Jerusalem's own. And the shallow storefront displays reminded me of those that filled the East (which had, in fact, been part of Jordan from 1948 until 1967), packed tight with cheaply made polyester dresses and shirts, and watched over by male shopkeepers who hovered in the doorways smoking cigarettes and looking weary but genteel in their cardigans and polished shoes. There were few women on the street and none at all, aside from me, in our hotel, the Palace (or Balace, in the local parlance), a clean if tired establishment, with a formerly opulent upstairs lobby, whose walls were covered with hazy mirrors and floors with worn carpets. From the ceiling hung a few dusty chandeliers, and behind the reception desk was an elegant dark-wood switchboard that seemed no longer to function but bestowed on the whole room the dated though still-vital air of a scratchy Bogart film, a cross between *Casablanca* and *Key Largo,* perhaps. When we checked in, the limping, gray-haired porter offered to take our single light bag, and as we rode with him in the creaky elevator up to our room he asked us where we came from. "Al Quds," Peter answered — the Arabic name for Jerusalem — and the old man's face lit up. *Mumtaz!* he said. *Excellent!* and began to rattle off the names of neighborhoods in a city that he either remembered from long ago or that had assumed, through hearsay, the more potent function of myth. He intoned: *Talbieh! Bak'a! Ras al Amud! Katamon!* . . .

We wandered on foot for hours that night, past more Roman ruins, clothing stores, and *shwarma* stands, and eventually came to peer down on the street below from a tea shop that turned out to be a men's club — a high-ceilinged, second-floor hall where round-bellied packs of middle-aged functionary types gathered to play backgammon and smoke the rented water pipes — though we hadn't realized the single-sex nature of the place until we had already climbed the stairs and stood framed in the doorway. I had begun to pull Peter away when a pomaded young waiter saw and rescued us. In one sustained gesture so gracious and balletic we couldn't help but follow obediently behind, he whisked us out onto a private balcony, prompted us gently, "Coffee?" then, before gliding off to fetch our tray, closed the double glass doors behind him, leaving us alone with our bird's-eye view of the busy intersection. We sat for a long time, watching the lights change, the crowds scurry, the buses lumber past, and by the time we found ourselves back on the sidewalk, I felt — perhaps presumptuously — at home on this little stretch, the shapes of whose shop fronts and signs had just impressed themselves on my mind in an indelible way. Whenever one travels this process takes place — the gradual, almost unaware replacement of expectation (our mind's-eye snapshot of the imagined city) with actuality (the concrete line and smell of the landscape before us). And in the case of Amman, which I had been warned by others was "ugly," "dull," "ordinary," I felt an attraction to exactly that plainness, the dog-eared, jostling quality of a real, lived-in, unsensational place. The longer we sat on those hard wooden chairs, the less vague Amman seemed, and the more I found I liked it.

The next morning, after waking in the dark to the blast of what sounded like a dozen next-door muezzins, we made our way down to a café where a gold-framed poster of Jerusalem's Dome of the Rock took up one whole wall. (No matter that our goal on coming here had been to escape Jerusalem for a brief while: At every turn in Amman, we were faced with shadow reminders of that other city.) There we ate an alarming breakfast of sweet cardamom coffee and even sweeter *kannafeh,* the cloying cheese pastry that I also knew from the East but that constituted, together with the hot, treacly drink, more sugar in one meal than I usually consume in the course of several weeks. Our heads buzzing, we flitted out into the street, determined to travel to a handful of sites that lay scattered to the south and east of Amman — the Umayyad desert castles, biblical Mount Nevo, the mosaic floors at Madaba. We flagged down a cab and asked the driver to take us to a bus station on the far side of town.

As we rode, around and around the crowded streets, Peter practiced his Arabic with the driver and I fixed my gaze out the window at the busy early-morning scene. At one point, we passed a long stretch of concrete, covered with a vividly painted mural that showed smiling families working the fields, riding donkeys, harvesting olives, and tending goats, and I understood somehow that the simple shapes and primary colors of this cinder-block idyll were meant to be Palestine, and that we were now circling or even passing through a refugee camp. It was an almost unconscious awareness on my part, since I had never seen such a place before and could not read the signs that might have announced where we were. But there was something about the fairy-tale intensity of the painted scene that told me.

We had arrived at the bus terminal, though when Peter asked the cab driver where we should go to catch the bus we needed, the man explained something rapidly in his own language. Peter translated for me: We had come to the wrong place. There was no bus from here to the mountains or desert. What would we do? We thought for a minute, as the driver sat patiently, waiting for us to decide. (His name, I now read from the license on the glove compartment, was Mahmud Zatari, from the Arabic word for thyme which, when dried, crushed, mixed with sumac and sesame, and eaten with bread, becomes a salty-sweet staple of the Palestinian diet and also serves — together with the olive, fig, and sabra cactus — as an embodiment of the Arabs' tie to the land.) I could see Peter was glad for the chance to speak Arabic in a more extended way and, after performing a few hushed calculations, into which we factored his comfort with the driver as a conversational partner, he asked how much it would cost for Mahmud himself to take us to these sites. A perfunctory bit of bargaining followed — the initial price the driver had quoted was so reasonable it seemed almost petty to go through the motions of negotiation — then we all agreed on an amount and soon were speeding in his taxi on the two-lane highway that stretched out of town.

Peter and Mahmud, who was bearded and about my age, had grown comfortable with each other by now; at first, we'd tried to pass as Americans, but Mahmud understood immediately that we were also Israelis, and wouldn't have it otherwise. Peter moved up to the front seat and they talked easily as I half-listened, not understanding really, but calmed by the modest dips in the landscape and the steady *"na'am na'am na'am,"* the *"yes yes yes,"* of Mahmud's speech, which I took to mean that he and my husband were in basic agreement. I grasped a Hebrew cognate here and a politician's name there, as well as the phrase, spoken by Mahmud, *"Baladi Lydda"* (my home is Lydda), which made plain who he was, at least in a crude, demographic sense. The son of Palestinian refugees from 1948, I imagined, who'd fled that ancient town for Jordan. As far as I could tell, the subject of his particular history was intentionally left dangling at this point as Peter and Mahmud went on to discuss other, more general matters: King Hussein, tourism, the neighborhoods of Amman.

By now we had arrived at our first destination, Mount Nevo, the peak where, at the close of Deuteronomy, Moses dies, barred from entering the Promised Land as punishment for not defending God to his people when in the wilderness they complained: "Wherefore have ye made us to come up out of Egypt to bring us into this evil place? It is no place of seed, or of figs, or of vines, or of pomegranates; neither is there any water to drink." Instead he grew angry, that day, and struck a rock to draw water — the water of strife, it was called — and for this fit of rage found himself on Nevo condemned by God to die with the generation he had brought out of slavery, without ever setting foot in the much-longed-for Canaan: "For thou shalt see the land afar off; but thou shalt not go thither into the land which I give the children of Israel." Then, according to the midrash, "God kissed Moses and took away his soul with a kiss of the mouth, and God, if one might say so, wept."

Mahmud parked the car and prepared to sit and wait for us — tour guide he was not — though when Peter asked him if he wanted to come along, he looked startled but pleased, and admitted that yes, he would like that very much. Mount Nevo was just half an hour's drive from the city of his birth, but Mahmud had never been there before; in fact, he didn't know anything about this mountain or any of the other sites we visited that day, and Peter found himself in the delicate position of trying to explain to Mahmud what he knew about the history of this place in rudimentary Arabic as we crossed the parking lot. Nabi Musa, as Moses is known in Islam, was of course familiar to Mahmud, though the biblical story of his death seemed less so. He listened thoughtfully as Peter attempted an explanation, then we pressed up the steep path toward the ruins above, where the Franciscan Fathers had erected a large cross and chicken-coop

sort of structure to protect the mosaics — all that remained of
the Byzantine monastery that once dominated the summit.

On that day Mount Nevo was wild with a wind that seemed,
itself, almost biblical in its force. We could barely stand or hear
each other speak as we pushed toward the building and inside,
where the gusts whipped against the flimsy tin roof and rattled
the walls while we paced around the pale but well-kept mosaic
scenes of wine making. A German tour group sat on benches and
listened primly to their guide, and though his words echoed
inside the large room, they were all but drowned out by the ter-
rific din of gale-force winds against metal. Mahmud looked a
bit uncomfortable at first, clearly unused to the stilted hush of
museumgoing, made still odder in this case by the awesome,
amplified winds, so ferocious and unlike the polite quiet that held
inside. But he looked excited by the day's unexpected adventure.
He made the rounds with cautious curiosity, looking carefully at
each floor display as if intent on committing it to memory.

Once outside, in a light so thin and bright it hurt the eyes, we
pushed against the blasting air and forced ourselves onward
and up to the highest and outermost crag. From there we
looked out across the range at a view whose rather crushing
symbolic significance I'd already realized before the three of us
came to rest side by side, staring over at "the land afar off,"
Israel, or as Mahmud gasped, *"Phalasteen."* Then he blushed
and apologized, correcting himself: *"Isra'el."* Peter said that
there was no need, that perhaps it was both, and I stood in
silence, thinking it an unkind twist that this so-called promised
place, by any name, looked far more beautiful and pristine
from Mount Nevo than from inside its cluttered borders. But
all our words, spoken and silent, were swallowed up by the
demon wind, and finally when we could stand the raging blasts
no longer we walked back without speaking, across the foundations of the ruined monastery and down toward the parking

lot from which, tousled and a bit dazed by all we'd just seen and thought, we sped off toward lower ground.

And so we spent the day with Mahmud, tooling across the wide-open expanse, stopping first in the car-crammed town of Madaba, where a famous church-floor mosaic offered yet another view of the place we had been so keen to forget for a few days: a sixth-century map of ancient Palestine, its center dominated by the walls of Jerusalem and Church of the Holy Sepulchre. The principle at work was rapidly coming into focus. The farther we traveled from the actual place, the closer the mythic one became. (In another ironic twist, the map featured a fourteen-hundred-year-old rendering of a place marked "Lod also Lydda, also Diospolis.")

Then we set off in search of the Umayyad desert castles, whose picture-book name did not prepare me for the stark look of their straight, chalky walls and the no-frills nature of their design. The regal hut at al-Karanah, for instance, was carved with what turned out to be functional slits for circulation and defense. Like the ornate Dome of the Rock in Jerusalem, these plain-looking structures were built by some of Islam's earliest caliphs, men who had once been Bedouins and still felt a strong tie to the desert and its unbroken lines. According to the guidebook, these buildings once served as pleasure palaces, weekend getaways for the citified former tribesmen, and were surrounded in that period by artificial oases planted with lush vegetation and stocked with animals for hunting. But now no sign whatsoever remained of any green or antlered species. Not a date palm or a man-made stream or a lone gazelle, just the blank, sturdy walls of the boxy castles that sat alone, or appeared to spring up in the midst of this otherwise utter emptiness, a seemingly endless horizon of low desert shrubs and primeval rubble.

No longer waiting to be invited by Peter, Mahmud would bound out of the car and stride ahead a few steps to greet the kaffiyehed keeper of the site with an elaborate set of blessings and handshakes. Then he would wander inside with us, by now both the proud host and the fascinated guest. One of these isolated eighth-century constructions was a former bathhouse for the fast-living caliphs of the time, decorated with ceiling-to-floor frescoes of frolicking naked women and wild lions, all with the same popping eyes, and as we strolled around inside, peering up into the darkly painted corners, Mahmud (who had already explained to Peter that he was religious, but not as religious as, for example, his wife, Samira) wore a silly grin plastered across his face and cast tentative glances at the nude female forms on the walls, as he did so, repeating over and over, in loud English, ostensibly for the benefit of the blond busload of Scandinavian tourists who'd also wandered into the crumbling rooms: "Wonderful, wonderful!"

Back in the car I assembled three small string-cheese-and-sesame-bread sandwiches and handed them around. We drank water and continued along the same road, which would, if we followed it straight, lead us to the Iraqi border, a purely geographical fact that struck me as fantastical, otherworldly. To most Americans, myself included, Iraq doesn't seem a place accessible by car: It's a TV mirage, a real place, to be sure, but one so far off it has the quality of make-believe. To enter Iraq would be a trick reminiscent of *Sherlock Jr.*, where Buster Keaton's dreamy projectionist wanders onscreen midmovie. And for an Israeli, proximity to Iraq is figured most often in terms of Scud range, not taxi rides. Yet here we were, driving and driving right toward the border and away from home as dozens of huge semis roared past us on the road, carting supplies the same way.

We were not, though, going to cross over. Rather, we had fixed our sights on Azraq, the town where T. E. Lawrence set up headquarters in a black basalt castle and where Mahmud had driven in search of gasoline. Before we could enter the city limits, however, we were flagged down by a policeman. After protracted negotiation and a drawn-out ritual of license and registration-card transcription — which happened in Arabic too rushed for Peter to follow but which did include the repeated and rather nerve-wracking mention of the word *Israeli,* with frequent agitated gesticulation and worried looks cast by Mahmud in our direction — he was issued a ticket for traveling outside his taxi zone and we were at last allowed to go. Mahmud was clearly distressed by the meeting with the cop, and by the hefty fee he'd been asked to pay for venturing from his narrowly proscribed route. More subdued now, and also tired out by the day's extended adventure, we bought gas, gave up on seeing Lawrence's castle, and turned the car around in exhaustion, beginning the trip back along the same road, the only road for miles. The sun had grown strong and stayed that way, well into the afternoon, and the longer we drove, the foggier I felt. My head still hummed from the morning's excess sugar and the strong gusts and views of Mount Nevo, while my cheeks were flushed from the dry, hot light that poured inside the cab. At a certain point, I drifted off to sleep, to the sounds of Peter and Mahmud talking and laughing gently, like old friends. . . .

When I awoke, we were driving past an ugly, upscale suburb of Amman, and Peter relayed to me, in muted English, that Mahmud had invited us to come to his house for a late lunch — it was around three-thirty now — and he had accepted. Was this, did I think, the right response? Was Mahmud just being polite by asking or did he really want us to come? I checked the guidebook which went on in rather canned-sounding terms about the friendliness of the locals. But after a full day spent watching Mahmud's warm interactions with a series of perfect strangers, including the traffic cop, whom he had treated at first as a long-lost brother, it did seem to me that the idea of the outgoing, hospitable native was not just a fanciful Western caricature. We should go, I said, it would be rude to refuse, and soon we found ourselves pulling up at a dirty curb in the heart of the same area we had passed through this morning, the Wahdat refugee camp, Mahmud's home.

Although I understood that Mahmud was Palestinian and so, almost by definition, a refugee, it hadn't dawned on me until that very moment that he and his family lived in a camp. In truth, I must confess that I hadn't thought twice about where they lived. Amman was full of modest apartment houses and I suppose I must have assumed that the Zataris made their home in one of these. And thinking back, my uncharacteristic lack of curiosity startles me, and makes me suspect myself and my convenient smudging of what seem in retrospect to be the glaring particulars of their situation: The brief, muralistic premonition of the morning notwithstanding, I had simply never bothered to imagine a refugee camp or the people who dwelled there, except in the haziest terms. In the abstract, one can (and many do) speak in informed terms about the frustration, the lack of decent sewage, the crowding, the filth; one can read books and editorials, sympathize, watch documentaries, and wish for a sudden, miraculous end to the problem; but I for one could not, until the instant the car came to rest a few feet from their doorstep, even begin to fathom in tangible, human terms the wrenching blend of hope and sadness, fantasy and total despair that fills the air, as kerosene and cooking fumes, in a nowhere-place like Wahdat.

We had a few minutes to let sink in the mind-bending fact of where our day had led us, as Mahmud excused himself to go warn his wife we were coming. Meanwhile, we sat in the taxi and waited, across from a large mosque, slung with loudspeakers. We were almost too overwhelmed to speak.

For the eternity of a few quiet moments, we slouched in the taxi cab and stared out the window at _____? In an odd lapse of memory, the actual outline of Mahmud's block has been excised from my mind. I believe I was too surprised at having arrived there to absorb the shapes around me; looking back I can only recall that each car that inched past raised a clinging cloud of gritty dust on the narrow, unpaved street. Then Mahmud reappeared and invited us in, voluble and confident now, on his home turf, and we followed behind him to the battered tin gate that marked the entrance to their miniature concrete courtyard. With her strong laugh and round face, full-moon-like under her white head scarf, Samira greeted us at the door and welcomed us — "my Israeli friends," as Mahmud announced us — with such cheer and force, she might have been my grandmother (though it turned out she was also exactly my age), ordering us to come in, sit close to the heater. When we entered the freezing-cold hallway of an apartment — two narrow, dingy, morguelike rooms and a closet-sized kitchen — she switched the TV from the Imam's wail to a dubbed Syrian cartoon that seemed to be set in colonial America, and began to shift the mound of blankets piled on top of the two mattresses that served, together with the old refrigerator and large television set, as the room's sole furnishings. The blanket heap turned out to contain her three napping children, whom she had stacked one on top of the other to keep warm. Immediately after our entry she whisked off to change out of her leggings and blouse into a more modest floor-length housedress of green velour, and returned, a ring on each finger, ordering us brusquely to sit still closer to the heater while she went to prepare our late-afternoon lunch.

Samira controlled the household, but Mahmud commanded a certain kingly aspect as he sat cross-legged on the mattress, smoking cigarette after cigarette, while he and Peter talked, I pantomimed participation, and his children climbed over him as he kissed them again and again. There were two little boys and an older girl, Noor, about five and named for the queen, King Hussein's strapping, American-born wife. Noor Zatari, on the other hand, was a pallid, skinny child with black brows that emphasized the transparent veneer of her skin. She fled into the other room when we entered then emerged a few minutes later, barefoot on the icy floors and with a hacking cough to show for it, but newly adorned in a red party dress, unzipped at the back. She stood in shy wonder behind the bedroom door and stared at me and my wool jacket, playing a stern game of peekaboo whenever I tried to speak to her in my primitive non-Arabic.

We could smell and hear frying from the kitchen hot plate, and within minutes Samira swooped back into the room with a large tin kettle of hot sage tea, which she ordered Mahmud to pour. Then out came a tray of savory potato pancakes, green olives, and three individual yogurt containers, each with its tinfoil lid folded back neatly and a spoon sticking out at a careful, upright angle. *Eat!* she commanded. We ate, and found that this poor man's feast was not just generous but delicious. "Tasty" was, luckily, one of the few words I could conjure from my minuscule Arabic vocabulary, and I repeated it like a mantra when Samira had finished cooking the first four or so batches of chewy pancakes and marched back in the room to plunk herself down on the cold floor and watch us eat her food. *Eat more!* she urged, almost accusing, and I did my best to oblige her, though by the time this last round of pancakes emerged from the kitchen I was so full I felt queasy. Still I continued to eat — just as lavish hospitality was expected of our hosts in this context, so I understood that gorging oneself to the point of discomfort was the responsibility of every good guest. Mahmud continued to pour more and more of the sharp-sweet amber tea while Samira, who waved away the suggestion that she herself try some of the food (she had already eaten, she insisted) chatted in an emphatic flurry, obviously relieved to find herself in adult company after a day spent alone with the children and the Imam in these frigid rooms. She would spring up periodically to introduce us to the latest family member to wander past. In the course of the few hours we sat there, some four or five brothers, cousins, nephews dropped by and stood at the door as they gaped at the "Israeli" visitors.

And in between the niceties, in the full-bellied flush that followed the meal, Peter and Mahmud progressed from meandering talk of soccer and basketball to a quicker and more intent exchange about the Zataris' life here in Wahdat. It was only later that Peter related to me exactly what they had said, though perched near the floor there, my legs tucked beneath me to keep from freezing, I understood that the conversation had modulated key in some important way, and I nodded dumbly as they spoke, as if I did in fact understand. Samira, for her part, would listen in silence then explode in a volley of words far tougher sounding than Mahmud's own. In my nonverbal estimation, she seemed like the friendliest sort of hard-liner. As it turned out, though, she was more like the friendliest sort of pragmatist. In the strong tones that came most naturally to her, she related her businesslike understanding of the inner workings of UNRWA health clinics, food subsidies, and nursery schools. Peter asked her questions — about medical costs, length of the school day, and so forth, and she answered in the expert tones of a woman who has made an ambitious professional career of home economics. Samira had, she explained with slightly bossy pride, been enrolled at a local college when she met Mahmud. He had also been a student there and was learning about computers. They had married and started a family and been forced by circumstance to put aside their studies — which, after all, cost money. Mahmud started driving a cab but wanted, he said, to return to school. "Someday," he smiled. "*Insha'alla.* Someday I will go back to college. Someday I will finish my degree," he promised us and himself, and the discussion continued in the same hopeful future tense, to the subject we had been tiptoeing around since we entered these dank rooms — Palestine.

"Tell me," insisted Samira. "Is it beautiful in Palestine?"

"Yes —" Peter paused. "It *is* beautiful there. Very beautiful."

"Mmm." She bobbed her head in a no-nonsense way, apparently content with his answer. "This is what we have heard, that Palestine is the most beautiful place. Much more beautiful than Jordan."

"Well, it actually looks very much like Jordan, which is also beautiful. But Israel is more developed."

She clicked her tongue as if to chase away this thought, and sighed.

Now Peter licked his lips and asked carefully, checking each word before he uttered it: "What will you do if there is a Palestinian state declared in the West Bank and Gaza? Will you move there? Will you take your family, leave Jordan, and go?"

"No!" Mahmud shook his head without guile, his voice sure, still smiling. "When there is peace, we will all be allowed to go back to our homes. We will return to my father's house in Lydda. That is what peace means, yes?"

My husband was, I think, overwhelmed by the directness and naive faith of Mahmud's answer and could not respond to his rhetorical question about the meaning of peace. Neither could he bring himself to announce that Lydda, Lod in Hebrew, now housed a Jewish slum, many ticky-tacky banquet halls, and Ben-Gurion International Airport. . . . Mahmud's father, who lived (Samira told us) upstairs, would probably no longer recognize the town that he and his children had spent the last half century dreaming of so fervently. The place he remembered simply no longer existed.

None of this talk was accusatory. In fact, part of what made the long afternoon we spent with the Zataris so powerful, unnerving, and bittersweet was the soft, seemingly schizoid way Mahmud had of describing his political aspirations in the utopian abstract as he lavished his hard-earned food and abundant goodwill on us, two American-Jewish Israelis, in the dimming light of that midwinter Wahdat dusk. He also didn't appear anxious to belabor the point about his father's house: Either his belief in imminent return was so strong it did not demand elaboration or else perhaps he knew deep down that now the situation was more complicated, that he might not ever see that house, that it might not even be standing. Without any fanfare he turned the topic from Palestine to his prized possession, a wallet-sized portrait of his oldest boy, glued down at the center of a wooden birdhouse construction and sprinkled with a child's fistful of silver glitter.

Peter, I could see, was starting to flag under both the social and linguistic strain of the extended day. Understanding that Mahmud and Samira must also be tired, we began to make signs that it was time for us to go, but before we could hoist ourselves from our stiff mattress positions, Samira leapt up once more, her eyes shining, and said she had a special treat for dessert, in honor of the guests. A delicacy! _____ — she gave the Arabic name, which Peter did not know. Mahmud's eyes were also glowing now with a kind of sybaritic fervor, and he agreed excitedly, *Yes, yes, let's have* _____! Noor and the older boy jumped up and down, *Yes, Mommy, yes!* _____! Even the baby seemed happy at the thought, or pleased by the sight of his brother, sister, mother, and father grinning all together.

So, once again, Samira withdrew to the kitchen in a rush and once again the sound and smell preceded the arrival of the food, which of course I recognized right away, though I feigned innocence until the moment she emerged triumphant a few minutes later, bearing the ultimate peace offering: an outsized aluminum tray arrayed with an individual cardboard bowl for every one of us, each filled to spilling with the most poignant popcorn I have ever eaten.

⟫⟨⟩⟨

It was dark by the time Mahmud dropped us near the Palace. As we sat beneath the dim car-light in his taxicab, saying our good-byes, he fished from the glove compartment an old business card emblazoned with a bird's face in grave, beaky profile (this card was not his own, but had apparently been left by a friend employed by the FALCON SUPERDELUXE HOTEL) and on the back, in neat ballpoint letters, he inscribed his name, address, and telephone number. We should call, we should come visit again, we should stay in touch. Peter pulled a few bills from his pocket to pay Mahmud the fare we had agreed on earlier in the day, when he was still a stranger, along with money to cover the traffic fine he'd received on our account — but the sum now seemed paltry, piddling in relation to all that Mahmud had given us, and even as I resolved to send the family a gift (T-shirts for the children? stuffed animals? slippers to protect their feet from the cold concrete floors?) I realized that this gesture too would be inadequate, possibly even insulting. Samira might see it as charity, a condescending token.

"God give you health," said Peter.

"May He give *you* health," answered Mahmud.

"And to your family," Peter returned, in response to which Mahmud rattled off a longer, more intricate wish that God grant us His graciousness, mercy, and protection.

Peter, still a bit shaky in the elaborately proscribed realm of Arabic greetings and farewells, responded with the all-purpose ". . . in peace."

There was, then, nothing to do except get out of the cab, wave good-bye, turn, and walk slowly up to the room we would leave behind the next day and never see again, but whose memory, like that of Mahmud, would remain with us as an echo of what might be, what might have been, redoubling across the divide.

HOUSE OF WINDOWS

xxxxxxxxxxxxxxxxxxxxxxxxxxxxxxxxxxxxxxxxxx

it was friday, half an hour before the pre-Sabbath siren wail, when I realized we had no olive oil. We had drained our last bottle down to the murky dregs and all the stores were closed.

Maybe Benny would sell us some from his stash. This stocky little jester of a Scottish antiquities dealer lived downstairs from Mazal, on the chilly ground floor of a grand house whose lintel was marked

1896
אתקנז

In addition to the several Near Eastern languages that our neighbor the Glasgow native had acquired over the years, he had adopted the local tribal custom of leaving his wife at home to handle the children while he wandered elsewhere — to our house, for instance — where he would stride, often barefoot, onto our porch, smile rakishly at me, then greet my husband through a toothy grin in gutter Arabic and offer up a duty-free cigar, brought back from one of his frequent trips to visit a Swiss collector or German curator. A sly wit, with a disconcerting knack for shifting from broad teasing to utter seriousness in a flash (his brooding deadpan made it hard to distinguish the two), Benny's jokes were swift and clever, spiked with salty entendre. His elastic English came as a tremendous relief after the thin, even broken, idiom that one heard from the mouths of so many native English speakers who had lived in Israel for years and lazily let their own language slip. Being in this place for an extended period, I had begun to doubt the sharpness of my mother tongue (prepositions were the first thing to go, with practical nouns close behind), and I liked talking with Benny, as a way of keeping linguistically fit. He was also quite knowledgeable — an expert on ancient seals, he wrote articles for museum catalogues and helped to assemble important exhibits — yet with his ruddy coloring, leathery hands, worn T-shirt, and unceremonious air, he could have passed for a day laborer.

In addition to his messy but priceless basement cache of dainty, dotted Phoenician pots, almond-eyed ancient Egyptian death masks, and jumbled piles upon piles of Ottoman seals, Roman coins, and early Christian signet rings (all of which he handled as carefully as he might a heap of mismatched Tupperware or pocket of spare change), I knew Benny had a jerry can of especially pungent olive oil that he'd picked up on one of his drives to Jericho. He would go there to sit, drink thick coffee, and swap dirty jokes in his broguish Palestinian dialect with his colleagues and clients, "gentlemen of the Oriental persuasion" as he called them. This was how he operated, bringing back from these West Bank sojourns either bids to do business of some obscure (to me) buying-selling-middleman-playing type or — what mattered more on this particular day — large plastic vats of hand-ground *tehina* and full tanks of green oil, collected as edible down payment or in place of change.

Peter, meanwhile, had spent the past hour watering and tending the garden across the street in a final weedy rush before the horn sounded and such work became taboo in the neighbors' yard. By now I was a bit desperate: Could he please go ask Benny if we could buy some oil? This was still early in our friendship with Benny, when our neighbor would address himself in a raucous, man-to-man way to Peter, and turn to me in a more restrained, even chivalrous, manner. Since then, he had relaxed in my presence, but at that point I didn't feel I could ask for the oil myself.

"Not now," Peter yawned, stretching out across the couch in end-of-the-week exhaustion.

"I can't make dinner otherwise —" I started to whine, but he had already dwindled off into his catnap and I was left alone with the impending darkness and my empty oil bottle.

Of course there was still the most obvious solution — at once the simplest (physically) and most complicated (emotionally). I put on a sweater, collected my keys, and left the apartment as quietly as I could, turning downhill at the doorstep, away from town, and past the so-called House of Windows. This elusive structure sat at the foot of our street, its rear facade studded with no less than three dozen irregularly sized and staggered openings, each commanding what I imagined must be its own singular view, or views. Part of the odd demeanor of this hundred-year-old apartment building, though, came from the apparent absence, behind those panes, of peering eyes. No matter how many trips I made past that wall of windows, I never once glimpsed anyone looking out, or caught the back of a head turning away. At the same time, I had the definite sense as I moved by those stone arches, like thirty-six raised eyebrows, that *the house itself was staring,* keeping a steady, unblinking watch over the scene below and all those who came and went with the years. No one knew exactly why the building looked this way — if the (anonymous) architect had meant these apertures as quirky, light-giving ornament, or if he had intended for the windows to serve some other, now-forgotten function. One friend speculated that the place had been fashioned as a monastery and that each window belonged to a separate cell. His guess was reasonable (it was right next door to the Silesian Sisters' convent and day school) but incorrect, so far as I knew. The rather ordinary domestic floor plan of the house appeared in most books about Jerusalem architecture; according to the vague characterizations in these guides, the shape and placement of the windows on the rear facade were of "particular interest," but that was all . . . there were no cells or other obvious clues to the logic of its design. Rather, at the front, an outdoor staircase led up to a landing that branched into corridors on the right and left, off which sat several spacious, symmetrical rooms. (Facing the house from that graceful but more ordinary angle, one would never know of its peculiar backside.) Windows there were aplenty, but no building nearby was more opaque.

The dimming light would soon melt into dark. Walking faster now, I proceeded a few short streets east, past the old men shuffling to synagogue and their grandchildren playing in the road, toward the highway that marked the unofficial but very real border between the two halves of the city, Jewish and Arab. The stoplight there brought an end to Musrara, our neighborhood, and a start to Musrara, the mirror neighborhood on the other side.

✕✦✦✕

Before this road existed, the space between Musrara and Musrara was no-man's-land, separating Israel from Jordan, and though the sandbags and soldiers had been gone for exactly the length of my lifetime, I still felt I was crossing a border — one that was, in its very nebulousness, trickier to navigate than an official checkpoint like that at Beit She'an. One passed over, without documents, as through Alice's looking glass.

The two neighborhoods went by the same name, and at this

hour the swifts darted indiscriminately over both. But one was here and one was there, and despite the politicians' rhetoric that pretended this city was "united," when I stood waiting to cross the six-lane swath of asphalt that ran between the East and the West it was plain to me as the giddy gold of the mosque's dome that I was poised to leave one universe and enter into another. In an exaggerated version of the process that took place every time I passed over the threshold of my own house and out into the world, I was entering someone else's city now, in this case, a place at once next door and galaxies away. (Some of what I describe is subjective, some not: When, in early September, the clocks are moved back an hour in Israel to mark the start of "winter time" they aren't yet changed over there, in the East, so that for a few absurdist weeks one can literally cross the street and find oneself in another time zone, in effect another season, where summer evenings linger on in the light.) Unlike most of our Israeli friends who hadn't ventured east since the intifada started in 1987, I wasn't scared there — and we would go often, to eat hummus, to wander and buy vegetables or olive oil, as I was about to do now — but I was aware, too, and not especially eager to rid myself of the sense, that the East would always remain for me a little strange, necessarily foreign. As I walked there I carried myself differently, with the light step and quiet tones of a trespasser, an interloper with the good fortune and means to travel abroad just to buy olive oil to dress her weekend salad.

Half a century before, the east and west of Musrara had been a single neighborhood. There were stories I'd heard about how, in 1948, in the days just after the Palestinian residents of the houses on what was soon to be the Israeli side had fled in fear for their lives — some left beds unmade and food on the table or even cooking on the stove where it burned to black — a few had tried to sneak back across the border at night to collect their belongings. There were also apocryphal tales of fortunes buried beneath the colorful floor tiles, and more plausible mention of Jewish treasure hunters who had looted drawers, taken paintings and pianos, and even dug up those tiles, in search of the riches they imagined were hidden underfoot.

One personal history I read described the anguish of a well-known Palestinian doctor and his German wife who were forced to abandon the house they had built in Musrara some thirty-five years before. Their children were all safe, studying in Europe and Beirut, but after the third floor of their home was demolished by a direct mortar hit, they had no choice but to pack a bag each and go. That this man was at the time also the foremost scholar of Palestinian folk amulets seems especially ironic. Realizing that war was inevitable, he had managed to box and transport to safety his substantial collection of brass and silver talismans, wolf's-tooth pendants, paper charms, glass beads, gilded garlic, tortoiseshell and hedgehog-fur cradle ornaments, dried cow's eyes, and "fear cups," the magical bowls believed to heal — though not even his possession of some fourteen hundred lucky pieces could hold the evil eye at bay: Every day after they fled to the small room the Greek Orthodox Patriarch provided them in the Old City (where the doctor lived with his wife, sister, and sister-in-law, and from which he continued to operate his clinic), the couple would climb to the top of the ramparts and look across at the sight of their private library being ransacked, their Biedermeier furniture loaded into trucks and taken away. From this helpless vantage point the couple also watched as their house was torched and burned to the ground.

According to other accounts from the period, the Jewish immigrants who were sent by the Israeli government to occupy these badly damaged houses in the months after the Arab exodus ended and the wartime shelling stopped often slept on the mattresses and kept their clothes in the standing closets left behind by the refugees. Our house was one of these houses, and these immigrants were our neighbors. And although our furniture was all our own, and the apartment's mortgage was listed in our name, I knew our house had other owners, somewhere in the world. Who? Where? Meeting Samira and Mahmud had made tangible for me the unsettling fact that I'd known before but had kept until that time conveniently general: *Somewhere* — they could be abroad or even just a few blocks away, exiled to the other Musrara — there probably lived a family who carried the memory of our house with them always, like one of the doctor's talismans. Or was it a constant, aching regret, like the long-ago loss of a newborn child? What, I wondered, had become of the people who had eaten meals and laughed and argued and powdered their noses in these rooms, who'd awakened facing these ceilings? Had they left in a rush or did they pack and go earlier, taking their trunks and valuables with them, as if for a long vacation?

Our neighbor Rafi still paid key money, a Levantine sort of lifelong maintenance fee, to an eighty-five-year-old Armenian lawyer who represented his building's original Greek Cypriot landlords (unlike the Arabs, the Greeks who had fled were not considered "enemies" by the state, so families like this one had been allowed to maintain pre-1948 ownership of their houses in West Jerusalem), and on the day when I summoned the nerve to approach City Hall and request information about our house's former owners, Rafi also appeared on the second floor, limping more severely than usual, took a number, and sat down for the long wait. Sweating and shifting his gaze anxiously, he explained that since his mother's death a few months earlier, her part of their shared apartment had come under dispute. The same Greeks owned these rooms, including the kitchen, with its Old World pantry and painted wooden cabinets, and though Rafi wanted to pay extra to keep the place to himself, there seemed to be a problem. He had come to find certain documents that might bolster his claims to the property. "And what are *you* doing here?" he asked, in the clipped but able English with which he liked to address me when I brought him a day-old *Jerusalem Post* so that he could practice reading from left to right. I answered that I was curious about our house's history. My curiosity, though, got little more than a blank look from Rafi, who steered the conversation distractedly back to Hebrew and his own troubles: Since his mother died, it was hard for him to get by, he said. He ordered food from a caterer, had a cleaning woman come twice a week, and managed to do his own laundry, but things were hard, very hard for a man without a wife. I listened and nodded as Rafi went on with his monologue, a more emotional version of which Peter had already heard from Rafi and recounted for me. When the older man talked to Peter in private he admitted he would like to marry but "wasn't in demand" and, turning the subject back to his late mother, began very softly to weep.

After I sat for forty-five minutes with Rafi, my nerves rubbed thin by the harsh fluorescent light and synthetic chill of the air conditioning, one of the blue-jeans-and-sandals-wearing bureaucrats wandered from the room to which we and the small crowd around us were awaiting entry, and mumbled with an indifferent clerical shrug that the workers were on strike. We should come back some other time.

I returned a few days later, took another deli-styled number, and found, after a full-hour wait, that a work slowdown was still in effect and that only one clerk was receiving the public. (The public, at that particular moment, consisted of an agitated-seeming group of ultra-Orthodox men, pacing in long black coats far too heavy for the season, one sleepy young woman in a low-cut dress, and what appeared to be most of the older male members of a family of Palestinians peasants, who hud-

dled and whispered among themselves.) Disgusted by the fruitless loss of another morning's worktime, I descended to the city
archive and sat, thumbing through old guides to the Holy Land
— *Baedeker's Manuel du voyageur: Palestine et Syrie; Cook's
Traveller's Handbook; Piccola Guida di Terra Santa* — all in
neat little leather-bound volumes and filled with ads for first-
class bookbinding, lantern slides, oil soaps, mother-of-pearl
beads, dental surgeons, perfume, attorneys-at-law, tobac-
conists, and sweet shops. I'd heard more than once that our
house had been a hotel "in the time of the British," as our
neighbors called the period of English military rule and the
League of Nations Mandate that followed, between December
1917 and May 1948, and I skimmed the names of the establishments listed, in the hope of finding some clue about our
house. . . . In 1926, *Le Guide Sam, Annuaire de l'Orient* —
sponsored by Cigarettes Salonica and featuring separate chap-
ters detailing the tourist attractions and shopping possibilities
along the train and steamer route from France to *Italie, Syrie,
Grèce, Turquie, Egypte, Bulgarie,* and last but not least
Palestine — listed six hotels and pensions: the Central, the
Allenby, the Grand New Hotel, l'Hôtel Saint John, Hotellerie
Casanova, and Pension Dominique *("près le Cinéma Sion"),* all
of which either sounded too grand ("150 Bedrooms, rooms
with private baths and running hand water. Music at tea and
dinner. Small dance every Saturday") or had addresses that didn't
match up with our own, though I realized that our street name
itself must have been different in those not-so-distant days.
Several old maps of a pastoral place called El Misrara revealed
that Tribes of Israel Street was then referred to as Saint Paul's
Road, Elisha Street was named for the crusader king Baldwin I,
and Ayin Khet, the grand boulevard below, was formerly
known as Godfrey de Bouillon Street, for Baldwin's royal
brother. I could make out our own house on these maps — as

well as the two trees, storage shack, and courtyard that once stood in place of our balcony and the neighbor's flagstone-paved entry — but the alley where we lived was too small to be marked with a name.

Even after a trip to the map room at the National Library, our street's former name remained uncertain. It was midsummer and hot when I went there to investigate, and the frantic blast of all the building's air conditioners had created what might be called Water Music, the noisy drip-drip of indoor "rain" slamming steadily into the dozen plastic buckets that the patient but haggard-looking librarian and her bespectacled little son were juggling, in a rather futile attempt to protect this room and its irreplaceable contents from the deluge. As I sat, tracing a finger along the tiny thread of ink that represented our alleyway on the Survey of Egypt Map from 1925, the mother-and-son team worked methodically, swabbing the floor with grayish rags, and large drops smacked down on the table alongside me. So, too, the 1926 plan of Jerusalem-Palestine, "Drawn and Heliozineographed at the Ordnance Survey Office, Southampton," was threatened by the steady shower that fell from the ceiling. I hunched over the map, to protect it from the moisture, and again saw that the careful British surveyors had rendered our house immaculately, right down to the stone staircase that led up to our neighbors' apartments, but that the street still had no name. I folded the canvas gingerly and left as fast as I could, wishing to speed the return of these precious documents back to their dry storage drawers.

As it turned out, the amiable grandmother of a librarian at the City Hall archive was also the keeper of municipal building records, though the information she possessed proved quite scanty and its trail vanished completely in the late thirties, well after our house's construction. There was no mention whatsoever of Ottoman-era permits, and while she let me flip through the worn ledger books from the early forties, in which block and plot numbers were listed in scrawled Hebrew longhand alongside the petitioner's name and address, there was no trace of our house there, nor of any other nearby. The only structure listed in our neighborhood was a movie theater, to be erected in the Russian Compound, where the City Hall and archive themselves now stand. Whether these plans were ever realized, I do not know. No sign of a picture palace exists there today.

When I asked the librarian if the shelves contained any additional material about older buildings, she gave me a look that fused amusement and annoyance. All the others who had come to request information were contractors with cell phones clipped to their belts, paint-speckled work boots, and an impatient air. The demands they made of her were simple and curt; it seemed my questions fell outside her area of bureaucratic expertise. As if to humor me, or get me off her hands, she waved me down the hall to the director of the archive, a white-haired, clip-bearded man named Yehezkel, who was sitting alone and apparently bored in his office, eating a bag lunch that let off a garlicky stink. His face lit up when I asked about Musrara, and I wondered how long it had been since someone had tapped on his door with a genuine historical, nonadministrative request. Unfortunately — he told me through an excited, smelly grin — there were almost no records available about the Ottoman period. He did, however, have a book filled with aerial photos of "the Land of Israel," as he called the country then known as Palestine, taken by English fliers at the end of World War I. Pushing aside his sandwich, he thumbed through, found the right page, and placed before me a slightly foggy picture, in which a tight cluster of tile-roofed buildings was visible from high above. "Do you see your house?" I thought so, though it was difficult to say for sure. The structures looked tiny in this snapshot, and many of my contemporary reference points were

absent, while other houses, now missing, crowded the miniature streets.

One day not long after my basically futile trip to the archive,
I passed our ponytailed and pedantic neighbor, Ophir, in the
street, and asked in an offhand way if he knew where I might
find information about the former owners, or the builders, of
our house. Though now I understood that he worked as an
architectural historian, when we first moved in Peter had asked
an old-timer neighbor what Ophir did for a living, to which the
answer had been the gruff and guileless "Ophir? He's a homo-
sexual." Ophir may indeed have been full-time, high-bitch gay,
but he, like the rest of the country, felt parenthood essential and
had recently adopted a two-year-old Indian orphan with dark
skin and terrified eyes. Since his son had arrived on the scene, he
had taken to addressing me in a crude stereotype of gossipy
female tones, as if his newfound role as single mother should
bring us hormonally closer. When I put my question to him, he
leaned over the handlebars of his little boy's carriage, clutched
the leash of his huge Doberman, Daphne, and gave a ladylike
grimace, as if a terrible scent had just welled up from the gutter.
"*Why —*" he pursed his lips and rolled his eyes. "*Why* would
you *possibly* want to know who built your house?" I mumbled
something vague about just being interested, to which he shook
his head firmly. "Your house has *no* distinguishing *architectural*
features, so why should it matter? *May-be* in Istanbul there are
records, but I don't know *why* you should care."

Though I'd played innocent when I questioned Ophir, in
truth I knew my answer might lie much closer than Istanbul —
just across the highway. Realizing that the *Through the
Looking Glass* principle was also in effect here, I decided to
walk to the East, to Orient House, the officially unofficial
Palestinian city hall or foreign ministry, where according to various newspaper accounts documents had been gathered in

preparation for the rather ominously dubbed Final Status stage of the peace talks, to prove pre-1948 Palestinian ownership of houses in neighborhoods like our own. No doubt the records there would stand in direct, contentious contrast to those in the West, with building and ownership from Ottoman times and through the Mandate charted, the books thinning out at about the time the records at the West Jerusalem archive thickened.

Before I set out for Orient House, I ordered microfilm copies of the library maps, and from the negatives, prints. When I arrived to pick up my pictures from the photo shop, just across the street from the burnt-out hull of the Eden movie theater, now a parking lot, the soft-jowled old Pole in the cotton shirt and suspenders behind the counter looked amused by the serpentine street-shapes he'd just seen, emerging from his chemical solution. "You're an archaeologist?" he asked, gesturing toward the maps, which were in fact considerably younger than he was.

"Something like that," I answered, and opened the envelope to find a trio of clear black-and-white cartographic renderings of the city, printed in peculiar, but somehow appropriate, reverse:

ЈEᴙUᴤAᴙEM

I could make out our neighborhood

AᴙAᴙᴢIM

as it was written, and when I held it up to the mirror and looked hard, the tiny rectangle of what would one day be our house — though at the time the map was made, it belonged to someone else. Who?

⟩⬥⬥⟨

Most every West Jerusalem institution has its poorer or more bellicose cousin in the East. So it is with the dingy bus station one passes after crossing the highway, and so with the Israeli

Ministry of the Interior. In the West this government office is housed in an unremarkable building in the center of town, and serves as the blandly annoying destination for all those in need of a passport, visa extension, or identity card. In the East, meanwhile, the ministry occupies a regular armed fortress, surrounded by an imposing steel corral, which serves as a literal and figurative means of keeping penned the huge, exhausted-looking crowd that has gathered there already in the middle of the night, waiting for the office to open come morning. This mass of men, women, and children will, on most days, stand for hours, condemned to wait in line for whatever the latest document the authorities have demanded they submit for scrutiny. While in the West, filling out official forms is usually no more than a paper-pushing irritation, in the East it can and often does become a matter of earth-shattering importance. Several years after I arrived in Jerusalem, a harsh Israeli policy had come into effect, engineered to preserve artificially a Jewish majority in Jerusalem: According to the new code, Palestinian families could be separated or denied permission to live in the city of their birth on the basis of claims filed at this office. In a bizarre, legalistic twist, all Palestinian Jerusalemites who refused to swear allegiance to the State of Israel, even those whose families had lived in the city for generations, were technically categorized as immigrants, and immigrants, at that, of a second-class sort, mere "permanent residents." Their rights to reside in the city, to travel, work, and receive social benefits, were dependent on their maintenance of this status. Once, proving residency was a fairly straightforward matter, though now, without any warning, the rules had suddenly changed, and the Powers That Be had grown suspicious. Even a brief trip abroad might jeopardize one's standing, as might the decision to spend a few years in a nearby town or country (a fairly common fact of life in scattered, post-1948 Palestinian society). If the ministry determined that one had failed to prove that one's home — or, in the perverse poetry of the law, one's "center of life" — existed in Jerusalem, one could be deported, or become, in essence, an illegal alien. And even when evidence was presented to the authorities in perfect order — in the form of water, electricity, and telephone bills, birth certificates, tax slips, leases or deeds to an apartment — it was sometimes not considered sufficient. At the whim of a ministry clerk, an identity card might be invalidated, shredded, or requisitioned and left for years in a hazy state of procedural limbo. As of this writing, various government ministers have issued various righteous-sounding statements about the need to end this policy, but for now, at least, the indignity remains on the books.

These unpredictable and punishing standards, it ought to be said, existed alongside an active campaign to woo Jews to settle in Israel, with the added incentive of special tax reductions, mortgage grants, and social service perks. One could, as a Jewish Israeli, travel abroad and stay there for thirty-five or even fifty years, then return and find one's citizenship perfectly intact, awaiting one with open arms, as it were. Indeed, the surreal flipside to the situation of the Palestinians in the East faced me when I went to apply for Israeli citizenship in the West and, after signing an affidavit that declared that I was a Jew of matrilineal descent, did not have tuberculosis, was not an alcoholic, and had never pledged myself to an enemy state, was calmly informed by the clerk behind the desk that there was no problem at all — even though my father, one Marvin Arthur Hoffman, born in Brooklyn, New York, on July 15, 1939, had been living in the Bak'a neighborhood of Jerusalem since 1957. "But — but I grew up with my father," I stammered, "in New Hampshire — and in Texas."

The clerk remained unmoved. "No, he's been here the whole time, but don't worry. It won't affect your application." My father's vital statistics did in fact match exactly those in the ministry's computers, except for the one rather crucial little detail of where he'd been living for the last three and a half decades. Apparently, when he entered Israel for a year as an idealistic young kibbutz volunteer and Hebrew teacher all those aeons ago, he was processed as a new immigrant and, according to the rather wishful thinking of the Zionist authorities, simply never left.

One lives in this city, if one is a Jewish Israeli of any conscience not strictly tribal, by learning to suppress awareness, to turn away in shame, disgust, or helplessness, hurrying on as the young soldier girls stationed before the central post office laugh and yawn and demand to see the papers of every tenth-generation Palestinian Jerusalemite who dares pass by on their way to work or shop. Many, of course, do not suppress but justify these policies with historical claims of self-defense, an attitude that may derive from some thin flickering filament of truth, the charged memory of a time and place where Jews were the underdogs, but which — when applied as it most often is here, with gross contempt for the rights and feelings of another people, for the big picture, in other words — has the ghoulish effect of turning the former victims into the present torturers. And one watches in horror as the same transformation, from sinned against to sinning, seizes many Palestinians who have suffered at the hands of Israeli bureaucrats or soldiers and who are also hobbled by a compulsive need to demonstrate that they can be just as heartless and authoritarian as any Shin Bet interrogator or bloodthirsty Hebron settler.

Even among those who recognize what is happening — the de facto implementation of municipal apartheid — and do object, whether by growing morose when they read the endless newspaper articles detailing these injustices and others more mundane but no less meaningful, such as the decision by the city to invest in a costly light rail system that will bypass completely the east side of town, or by expressing their dismay more vigorously and attending demonstrations, signing petitions, campaigning for human rights, or even just learning Arabic and honoring the language of its speakers, even *they* must work at some level to ignore what is happening in a minute-by-minute way, or simply boil over. Most Israelis are too distracted by their own problems and by the damage being done to the western side of the city to notice, for instance, a new law (or newly enforced old law), expressly designed to snuff out the business of the city's Palestinian vegetable sellers, and with it the once-bustling street life of the East. Needless to say, there are much more serious issues at stake there as well — such as an extreme shortage of housing and classroom space, and the cruel policy of denying medical treatment to those Palestinians whose Jerusalem residency is in doubt — but I choose this example both because it is something I have witnessed and can vouch for in the first person, and because it indicates in a more vivid way the nefarious and essentially racist processes at work, what Palestinian filmmaker Elia Suleiman meant perhaps when he called his fine and painful movie, about the fate of his people's culture, *The Chronicle of a Disappearance.*

Due to a combination of political and "security" considerations, the municipality has declared it illegal for Palestinian vegetable sellers to market their goods in the street. Until recently, the sidewalks and steps around the Damascus Gate were crowded with these peasants from nearby villages, mostly gruff-voiced women with rough hands and long, embroidered dresses, whose livelihood depended on the sale to passersby of their small seasonal crops — a pile of dark, stubby squash, a bowl filled with grape leaves, a small mound of okra, several loosely tied bundles of medicinal sage, dandelion greens, purslane. Taken aback, perhaps, by all that unruly color and motion, City Hall used its legal authority and a few lengths of bright green plastic to designate a "Peddlers' Market" in a sterile, newly constructed plaza that sits west of the heart of the East's mercantile center, and ordered the *fellaheen* to do their business there or nowhere at all. Though the commands were couched in predictably patronizing terms, as if moving the peasants to this cutoff, confined space were intended to improve their economic, civic, and sanitary lot, they themselves weren't fooled. Not surprisingly, the place is dead: Aside from the fact that one must walk well out of one's way to reach it, the setup feels creepy and unnatural, depressed, with the would-be decorative fountains often left dry and trash piling up all around. What East Jerusalem dweller in his right mind would want to do his shopping in this squalid pseudo-*shuk,* under the Big Brother–esque watch of a glaring detachment of Israeli Border Police? The mayor and his political cronies are not, I should point out, stupid: They know exactly how unappealing, how demoralizing the arrangement is, and hope that at some point the peasants will just give up, gather their heaps of peculiar unwaxed vegetables, and vanish over the Jordan. In this case, the opposite has taken place, as most of the sellers have simply rejected the rules and made their way back to the street where the army and police allow them to stay — for now, that is, until the next time some official feels a sudden restless urge to flex his municipal muscles and issues orders to vacate once again.

The same haphazard, bullying enforcement goes for alleged building violations, punished far more frequently and harshly in the East. In the West, what's another story on a new hotel? Nothing that can't be squeezed out of the mayor's office and city council in return for electoral favors or a hefty campaign donation. In the East, meanwhile, families will often apply for legal permits to build their own homes, and find their requests denied without cause. (In certain Arab parts of town, no one has been granted such a permit in more than thirty years.) Desperate for a place to live, the families will sometimes go ahead and build anyway, only to find the so-called Civil Administration's bulldozers at their front door, revving up to wreck it.

The signs of this slow but sure demolition of the city's native Arab presence and character do not, though, turn up only in the East. Almost every afternoon I stroll through the middle of West Jerusalem, where at a central stoplight two pink-stoned buildings face the road and an engraved dedication reads, in elegant, evenly proportioned English, Hebrew, and Arabic letters:

KING GEORGE V AVENUE
Opened by
His Excellency SIR HERBERT SAMUEL
High Commissioner for Palestine
in the presence of
SIR RONALD STORRS
Governor Jerusalem Jaffa District
RAGHEB BEY EL NASHASHIBI
Mayor of Jerusalem
9th December 1924

Except that now, one of these structures houses a neon-encircled, glatt-kosher Sbarro pizza joint, all paper plates and industrial grease, while across the street, the wall in which that delicate trilingual inscription is trapped belonged, for the years of the period in question, to a store committed solely to peddling Settler Merchandise. On the sides of this building, huge banners screamed, Chicken Little style:

JUDEA SAMARIA AND GAZA ARE HERE

(They are no such thing, of course. The loaded biblical terms are an insidious way of laying linguistic and therefore historical claim to the occupied West Bank and Palestinian-controlled Gaza Strip, both decidedly There.) Inside, one could purchase children's puzzles, dried flower arrangements, painted silk scarves, and the latest in catchy Revisionist bumper stickers, all presumably gift-wrapped in casual Arabrein ideology and colorful stick-on bows. One need not, I think, be nostalgic for the heyday of British colonialism to see this takeover of Jerusalem's main intersection by a group of pistol-packing messianists — a great many of them born in New Jersey or the Bronx — as grotesque in the extreme.

This search, then, for the other owners of our house was my modest and by no means ideal attempt to stave off that terrible, willed obliviousness I felt mounting inside me, at the same time that I hoped it might help me stifle the unbecoming urge to kick a hole in the window of the settler gift shop. Perhaps my motivations were selfish: I think I'd begun to fear for my imagination. What sort of mental and emotional atrophy might set in when I ceased to wonder who had come before me here, and who, or what, would follow?

There was also a more tangible and immediate dimension to my hunger to know more. Like most Israelis, my contact with Palestinians was limited almost entirely to the impersonal, extremely unbalanced realm of fleeting dealings with construction workers, waiters, janitors, and shopkeepers' assistants. We'd attended a few peace group meetings with Palestinian activists, though the willed, ambassadorial nature of these occasions, I found, precluded real closeness. First names, baklava, and sweet cardamom coffee were invariably passed around the room, and it rarely went beyond that. More recently, Peter's various Arabic teachers had widened the circle of our cross-cultural interactions in a small though meaningful way. For the first time ever, we had a few Palestinian friends. But instead of taking the edge off my curiosity, these new relationships only made me eager to push further into that other close-but-distant world, to make the abstractions concrete. And while I realized that my research project was a paltry gesture, no real weapon against the larger, darker, more general forces at work all around me, and one unlikely to matter in the slightest to the particular family of Palestinians concerned (their own relation to the house would not be affected by my discovery of their surname; I had no plans to turn over the deed to our home), it still seemed to me imperative to try to learn who they were — for my own sake. And even if I could do nothing practical with this knowledge, I could not agree to pretend not to care.

Ignoring the situation, meanwhile, is a luxury most Palestinians do not have, and when I passed by on my way to Orient House that scorching morning, around eighty-thirty, the throng outside the Ministry of the Interior was already enormous and desperate-looking in a muted though palpable way. Young boys with old men's faces wandered through and hawked ice cream from wooden boxes slung over their shoulders. Women in long dresses and head scarves held umbrellas high above the pushing crowd, in what appeared a futile attempt to keep cool. And on the sidewalk opposite, the usual fleet of self-employed scribes stood before their collapsible card tables, each armed with a manual typewriter and pad of forms, taking dictation and translating for those who could not write or answer the Hebrew questions alone. Aside from a jeep filled with helmet-and-nightstick-toting border policemen, I was the only Jew in sight, and a small path cleared before me as I passed through the crowd and alongside the High Life grocery store, a little treasure chest of a market run by Palestinians who had apparently spent time in the United States and whose English flowed, quick and colloquial. The store's shelves were filled with exotic European, Asian, and American items that never surfaced in Israel proper — Indian fish spices, tinned French chestnuts, blue-corn nacho chips, obscure Dutch beers, and the like. Though we often shopped there on Saturdays or in the late afternoon, when the ministry was closed and the street outside quiet, the place seemed different, more decadent on a weekday morning, with these weary, pushing crowds out front and its jolly name reduced to a stinging irony. The high life indeed!

Similar crowds usually spilled from the sidewalks before the American consulate, one street over, though the first time I went there, in search of an absentee ballot for a U.S. presidential election, I stood at length on the wrong line. Without thinking, I'd surveyed the two groups of people awaiting entry — one Israeli, one Palestinian — and gone automatically to take my place with the Israelis. Only after waiting patiently and for some time did it occur to me that the people around me, my ostensible countrymen, were filling out request forms for American tourist visas: They were planning to go to the country of my birth for vacation, or a few years of study. Meanwhile, the other line was not meant for Palestinians per se, but for American citizens, all of whom, in this particular instance, were Arabs, people whose country of birth was probably right here, but who held citizenship elsewhere — in Dubuque? Embarrassed, I switched lines and awaited my turn to enter.

Now, as I walked toward Orient House, I found myself metamorphosing, for convenience' sake, into an American, plain and simple — that is, more of an American than I'd ever felt myself when I lived in the United States, where I considered myself first of all a Jew. Several times I stopped to ask directions in English, and found I was inadvertently acting a chipper part, full of bright thanks and smiles.

By the time I got to Orient House, a quirky two-tiered structure whose slightly quaint, jewel-box design belies its serious function as the center of Palestinian political activity in Jerusalem, I had evolved completely, not just into a flag-saluting, milk-fed prairie dweller but an American Journalist. Perhaps my use of the disguise was hypocritical; as I moved toward the security booth, though, I chose to eat all the disparaging thoughts I'd had about journalists over the years and take advantage of the path the word would clear before me . . . and sure enough, when I announced myself a Reporter, I was waved inside the fancy wrought-iron gates by the rather baffled-looking guard who seemed brand new to the job and simply shrugged me through. And so I moved up the steps and across the black-and-white tiles of the checkered patio, passing the clusters of brawny young men with dark glasses and cell phones who dawdled on the stairs, chain-smoking and talking. Were they Palestinian police? According to the Oslo accords, their presence wasn't allowed in Jerusalem, though I was fairly certain that this was the tacit job description of most of the large, thuggy crew. They carried themselves in the officious manner of proud recruits who'd been vested with titles, equipment, and a certain cachet, but scant actual power, and when I entered the foyer and stood trying to figure out which hallway I should follow, several of them rushed to help. "Welcome? Welcome?" they chimed, and proceeded to lead me en masse to the appropriate door in broken English and with timid, almost girlish smiles. (This overenthusiastic reception stood in laughable contrast to the oblivious, take-a-number-and-rot situation at the busy West Jerusalem City Hall.) I had a sense that they'd been sitting idly for days on end and were thrilled at the chance to do something, anything to make themselves useful. The whole building seemed suspended in lazy limbo — clerks sat drowsily at their desks, sipping coffee, few ordinary citizens wandered the halls, and the air itself scarcely seemed to move — though in addition to the typical Middle Eastern slackening of bureaucratic pace that their inertia implied, I realized that this might be a charade orchestrated with skill for outsider eyes like

my own. Technically, Orient House was not supposed to operate in an official capacity, so that the *appearance* of inactivity
was probably being carefully cultivated, while real business
went on behind closed doors. I approached one of the secre-
taries and roused her from her trance.

Walid, she explained, was the man I needed to see, though
"Walid will not come here today." As she spoke, the pretty
young woman with the knot of gold chains at her throat and
thick, liver-colored lipstick eyed me warily from behind her
computer screen. An older man, a clerk or official in a tie and
cardigan, despite the heat, stood alongside her, also staring
skeptically at me as I spoke. I should come back tomorrow, she
said. In the morning. At nine o'clock. "You would care," she
ordered me with a question, "to leave your name and reason?"
In blocky letters I inscribed the point of my visit on the pink slip
of paper she provided, taking pains to sound as dispassionate
as possible. (I did not refer to "my" house.) Skimming what I'd
written, she now questioned with an assertion, apparently as
impatient as the policemen who loitered outside to be of some
active help. "It is the West Bank you are interested in," she
offered. "Settlements."

"Actually, it's West Jerusalem, one neighborhood there —"

She looked wary, and the man beside her continued to peer
grimly at me. "Yes. Walid will know of this."

"Great!" I heard myself saying, again in too chipper a tone.
"Great! I'll be back tomorrow." I gulped, smiled at both of
them, turned to go, and felt their eyes following me in suspicious silence as I moved down the empty corridor.

Walid, it turned out, was a bearish man with crisp, slightly formal English, a shock of prematurely graying hair, a gold wedding band, and firm handshake. He welcomed me into his cluttered office where a fan whirled near the window and asked, in

the friendliest and most businesslike tones I had heard anyone use since I'd entered Orient House, what he could do for me.

Almost before I had finished explaining that I was researching the history of Musrara, the history of several particular houses there, in fact, and I wanted to know if perhaps there might be records available, concerning home ownership or — Walid understood and had pulled a chair beside the metal bookcases that lined one whole wall, stood on tiptoe, and reached for a binder. "Here."

Now in a single, fluid gesture he adjusted the reading glasses that hung from a chain around his neck, sat down, opened the notebook, and began to flip quickly through the forms there, each filled out in careful Arabic longhand. "Claims," he explained, as he skimmed the pages. (He seemed like a man who needed little sleep to propel him through the taxing day.) Here, in neat plastic files, were the claims of hundreds of families who had lost their homes in Jerusalem, assembled with the help of the local *muhtars* who kept track of where everyone lived, or who knew that this one would have word of that one, and so on and on, through the radiating circles of Palestinian social life where, to hear Walid tell it, everyone knew everyone else, or at least their second cousin. "Now," he ordered me, affably. "Write this down —" and he began to list family names, telephone numbers. "The _____ family, they are from Musrara, and Dr. _____, a professor, you have heard of him, of course. Here is his phone number. And the _____ family, they will tell you who you need to talk to, who might know about this house. You will call them. But first, you will go to J_____," he decided for me, and his resolve came as a kind of relief. Though I had my own serious doubts about just what it was I was digging for here, Walid did not seem to share them, and his confidence was almost catching. "He had a house in Musrara. His cigarette shop is near here. You can walk on foot, I will draw you a map: beside the pharmacy, near the shoe shop, across from the post office, yes? You know? Good, he will talk to you. You will give him my name. He will give you the key."

The key. Walid's was a funny turn of figurative phrase, considering the cliché of the displaced Palestinian who holds fast to a literal house key in hopes of returning someday to the long-lost lock it implies. Less than ten minutes after entering Orient House, I found myself shooting down the street, a bit dazed at the names and numbers he'd just entrusted to me, without question, the reassuring sound of his last sentence — *he will give you the key, the key* — echoing in my ears.

When I reached the corner that Walid had marked with an X on his swiftly sketched map I began to walk more slowly, and noticed, as I went, that two or three other stores also shared the name J_____ — brothers or cousins. I found the tobacco shop easily, a tiny storefront I had passed numerous times before, its small window filled with cigar boxes, plastic lighters, and sun-bleached cartons of Marlboros.

Inside, the stale smell of sweet pipe tobacco was heavy and unmoving. There was little room inside the dim space to maneuver, and the presence of just two customers made the place feel cramped, still more airless. I was the only woman in the shop and I tried to stand as far off to the side as the narrow aisle would allow, while those before me — a stooped grandfather under a white kaffiyeh and a younger, bespectacled businessman in a jacket and tie — bought their cigarettes and exchanged niceties with the shopkeeper who attended to them somewhat stiffly from behind the glass counter. He was of indeterminate middle age, with a thickening waistline, a full mustache, and no apparent interest in acknowledging the presence of the strange female who had just entered his store. After a few minutes I realized that the old man in the kaffiyeh wasn't going anywhere (he seemed to have come here to lean and to chat) and that I would have to speak up or go on being ignored.

"Mr. J_____?" I began, a bit pinched in the throat.

"Yes," he had to admit, sullen, not quite making eye contact.

I went on in a rush to introduce myself, drop Walid's name, explain in broad terms the purpose of my visit, and ask if he might mind talking to me about Musrara.

There was silence. For a moment, he let his gaze flit across my face, as a searchlight checks the horizon for enemy planes, but then he pulled his stare back and looked vacantly at the counter before him, seemingly unmoved. "You don't want me," he announced, rather bored. "You want the Big J_____." Another glum, protracted pause. "My father. He is not here."

"Will he be here later?"

"Maybe."

Now I hesitated, unsure how to proceed. "Well, could I — would you mind if I came back later? When is a good time to come?"

"We will be busy later," the Little J_____ asserted, and this time he looked at me longer, with a steely and weirdly self-satisfied calm, as if I'd just let slip some crucial detail and given my *true* purpose (something wicked) away. While I meant, of course, to ask only the gentlest questions of the Big J_____, for an instant the son's deliberate look, his wary need to show me he meant to protect his father from my prying and everyone else's, made me mistrust myself in a deep and harrowing way: What was it, really, that I wanted from these people? And what did I mean by barging into this man's shop early on a hot summer morning and pummeling him with bitter historical questions, digging for fresh new adjectives about a time and place he would likely prefer to forget? By now, though, I'd come too far to turn back and though I realized that he did not mean to let me talk to his father — not today or ever — I offered, with a strained sort of cheer, to leave my name and phone number. "He can call me," I suggested, hopefully. "When he has time."

The Little J_____ took the piece of paper and inspected my nervous handwriting. "You live where?"

"In Musrara," and he nodded, as if I'd confirmed all his very worst suspicions. "Thank you," I tried to smile, at a loss for words. "Thank you very much," at which point I was already halfway out the door, desperate for the unambiguous glare of the street.

✕✦✦✕

Walid's list sat untouched in my notebook for months. The Big J_____ did not call, and I found I could bring myself neither to approach the shop again, in the hope of finding the older man there alone, nor pick up the phone and contact the families Walid had suggested. Every time I considered the prospect, the vinagered frown of the Little J_____ would surface in my mind and stop me in my tracks. I could not blame him, either, for the sour countenance he'd turned on me when I entered his store and begun to fire off my questions; if anything, I thought I understood it. (I'd even begun to wear this expression myself whenever I considered proceeding with my search.) And though I needed no external discouragement to keep me from following up on these various clues, the worsening political situation provided endless dismal opportunities to stall. The borders to the West Bank — where several of the families on Walid's list now lived — were often sealed off, the residents of certain towns placed under curfew. The army seemed to be everywhere, on a constant aggressive terrorist alert. Whether there was an actual beefing up of the "security forces" in Jerusalem or whether I'd simply become more conscious of their ubiquity I cannot honestly say, but the effect, either way, was wearing: Choppers flew low over our house on Friday mornings before midday prayers at the Al Aksa mosque, frequent sirens howled from the East, while all the *shuk* and downtown street corners were manned by groups of well-armed soldiers, just waiting for something to blow. One often had the anxious sense that their very visible, almost impatient presence would speed that process along.

In the meantime, too, I'd run headlong into another brick wall when I contacted a Palestinian-American journalist whose family had once lived in Musrara. After I read an impassioned article he wrote about walking past his paternal house and see-ing the wooden cabinets his grandfather had built tossed by the present-day Jewish tenants out on the stoop with the trash, I wrote him a letter and asked if he might be willing to speak to me. Of course, he dashed off a quick note: He'd be happy to help. He would bring his father, who remembered the place, to sit and talk to me — but not now, he was busy, getting married. Next month, perhaps. He would contact me. But that month passed, and another, and another, during which time I read in the paper that the main society of Palestinian journalists had forbidden its members from meeting with Israelis in any con-text not directly related to work. Did this ban, I wondered, apply to him? And me? I called once. He was sorry, right now it was not possible, maybe later, he explained loudly but politely into the muffled static of his cell phone, which seemed some-how to understand its role as hokey symbol of cross-cultural communicative difficulty and kept cutting out, making real talk impossible. I waited a while longer then wrote a note, to remind him, and one more — then I stopped. I had no desire to push. Whether he meant this constant postponement as a deliberate snub or was in fact just incredibly busy hardly seemed to mat-ter. The upshot was the same.

Bit by bit, my appetite for the project waned. It seemed to me now too frivolous and vague to pursue such a tack. What dif-ference did the history of our house make, given the shape of the current situation? What right did I have to force open this old can of worms? And what, I wondered, was I going to do if I ever found the house's former owners? Invite them over for coffee? When I told some Israeli friends in general terms what I was up to, they chuckled darkly and looked a little worried: Did I know, A. asked, that a couple in Lod had befriended the Palestinians who had once owned their house, first welcoming them in and serving them cake, then feeling a bit anxious at their frequent, unannounced visits, finally waking one morning to find the entire family encamped right on their front doorstep, luggage in tow? This case turned into a protracted, messy legal battle, he warned. This was not ancient history I was sifting through here. I should watch myself. I would watch myself, I promised. In the meantime, anyway, I'd nearly given up hope of ever learning more.

But then, in the least likely setting, all my meandering gumshoe work at last began to fall into startling place.

On the Isle of Skye, in the town of Portree, just as a thin scrim of late-August rain began very softly to fall, we ducked inside a bookshop and began to browse in satisfied silence. We hadn't left Israel in more than a year. Desperate to immerse ourselves in a different mental and physical landscape for a few weeks, we had journeyed by plane then train then ferry to this drizzly Scottish spot, as far from home as any we could imagine. The whole country seemed to our tourists' eyes cool, calm, wet, friendly, and filled with good bookstores. Just as Jerusalem had managed to kill off its final downtown movie theaters, no real bookstores remained there either, and whenever we traveled we wound up carting home a full suitcase of new volumes, as mountain dwellers might haul back to their isolated cabin a season's supply of canned food and beef jerky.

I was not searching for such a thing, of course, but there, amid the cookbooks, novels, and Gaelic ballad collections, I found myself grasping a smooth hardback whose cover registered before its title did. For a moment I thought I had hallucinated the dreamlike black-and-white photograph of a Highland military band, outfitted in kilts, knee socks, and army jackets, tooting their instruments before a bright hilltop view that was strangely familiar, unfocused in the distance but plain to me nevertheless, its identity confirmed by the pale pebbled texture of the ground that spread beneath the musicians' neatly buttoned spats and continued, flat and unmistakable, into the picture's foreground. A caption on the inside flap explained the unlikely meeting of costume and backdrop: "Scots regimental band, Jerusalem, 1937." I bought the book, *Mandate Days* by A. J. Sherman, and gobbled down its fascinating contents, a learned collage drawn from letters, diaries, and various other firsthand accounts of the lives of British civil servants, teachers, military officers in Palestine, 1918 through 1948. Summing up the paternalistic blend of attraction and repulsion that many of the English visitors to the country seemed to have felt, especially as the period of British rule stumbled to a close, one woman explained, "It could be such a lovely country if the people in it were different."

The book was brimming with live period particulars and comically supercilious, self-involved English voices, like that of the Nazareth assistant district commissioner's wife who wrote in a 1935 letter to her mother-in-law: "There was a General Strike here yesterday but the only effect it seemed to have was that the roads were delightfully free of traffic!! It was a protest by the Arabs against the 'so-called inactivity of the Government after it has been found that the Jews were smuggling in arms' — they are awful fools — I think the house is going to look very nice but none of the curtains are finished of course. . . ."

Others were more sympathetic in their frustrations — their sentiments, if not their haughty tone, understandable and still unnervingly apt, like the official who gives an eyewitness account of the bombing by future prime minister Menachem Begin's terrorist gang of the English army headquarters at the King David Hotel. The man's own deliverance from death took the unlikely form of a pink gin he'd paused to drink at the bar before proceeding to his business in the secretariat's wing, the eventual site of the blast. His surreal epistolary description builds through the "noise of smashing glass & wrecking furniture & . . . blackness," to a snooty sketch of the "crowds of screaming orientals (an unedifying sight!)," to the discovery that his driver has been killed. ("He was a Moslem. I feel his loss dreadfully.") Even his final stinging words, tinged with more than a hint of outright anti-Semitism, are still drawn from a well of feeling too deep to dismiss out of hand: "Considering," he concludes his long letter to his father, "we are really awfully well, all of us — but it will be grand when I leave Palestine and never have to speak to another Jew again — they have murdered too many of my friends."

Another officer's wife is more ecumenical in her contempt: "Everywhere one turns, even the holiest places," she writes, "are people struggling to get the better of each other — the different religious orders — the Arab — the Jew. One can quite imagine that it was here they crucified Him." And in addition to the blood-and-guts political sagas and lofty statements of disgust at the local manner, there are more banal but no less surprising descriptions — of the so-called Ramle Vale, a mounted hunt staged by a homesick inspector of police, with local jackals standing in for the usual English fox, and even of the cinemagoing habits of the English officers, who would sometimes find themselves stuck at the back of the theater in a pewlike box with a couple of necking strangers. One man described his discomfort: "There were occasions when I and another man were the unwilling intruders upon love's young dream, averting our eyes and sealing our ears with whatever discretion we could assume, but feeling that we were all too physically adjacent."

While these voices and anecdotes were all vivid and engaging, sometimes bleak, sad, or familiar in their despairing pitch, the book did not seem connected in any specific sense to my own unsolved mystery. Not, that is, until a few pages from the end and the mention of one John F. Spry, in 1947 the acting head of the Department of Land Registration, who "made extraordinary efforts to safeguard and photograph the massive registry books documenting ownership of property throughout Palestine." As the British prepared to withdraw from the newly partitioned country, Spry understood the danger to which these records (many dating back to the Ottoman era) would be subjected and rushed to arrange for pictures to be taken of the books, at the same time overseeing storage of the original copies in the Jerusalem YMCA.

Now the details came flooding, more details than I could have hoped: A footnote in Sherman's book sent me to the reading room of the National Library, where a journal article related with pointillistic care the exact make of the cameras that Jewish photographer Yosef Schweig and his assistants, both Arab and Jewish, used to carry out Spry's orders (a small Leica and three microphotography machines flown in specially by the RAF). And now I knew that as of November 17, 1947, there existed in Palestine 884 Ottoman Registers; 2,192 Registers of Deeds; 1,424 Registers of Title; 47 Registers of Writs and Orders; 690 Deeds Books; 1,906 compendiums of documents; and 247,600 files of unsettled lands. (Surely our house must be listed there, somewhere?) So, too, I read of the long, tedious, and physically elaborate process of photographing these heavy bound books and loose-leaf pages day after day at the besieged Public Information Office in the Palace Hotel, and of the trail the documents had followed afterward. The original books were eventually handed over to the Emergency Committee, a Jewish body organized to assume command over the various British offices as they shut down or ceased to function, although once the committee had taken physical control of the books, they found themselves stumped as to how to preserve this library of heavy volumes in the midst of a war. "Please lend a hand," wrote one desperate committee member to the Israeli Ministry of Justice, "to save the land books from the Jews." Meanwhile the backup microfilm was shipped, undeveloped, to London, where it was stored and then, starting in 1949, returned to Israel incrementally in the form of printed enlargements. By then the Jewish state had been declared — and with it a customs office, whose functionaries didn't hesitate to tax the shipments of local property records when they returned, carefully marked by English officials "Cinema Films." Finally, the article recounted that in February 1953, the remaining fourteen hundred rolls of film were returned to the director of land registration and land settlement at the Israeli Ministry of Justice, where the books themselves had also come to rest.

So that was it, the address to which I should have turned in the very first place, before Scotland, before the Little J_____, the busy journalist, Walid and his skeptical secretary, before the photo shop, the map room, Ophir, Yehezkel, the archive librarian, and the striking workers on the second floor of West Jerusalem's City Hall. I picked up a phone book, found the ministry's downtown address, and walked in five minutes to the office, which turned out to be located in an ugly firetrap of a skyscraper smack-dab at the center of town, one floor up from the salon of the gregarious former Bostonian who sometimes cut my hair.

Five minutes and fifty shekels later, I had before me a document, stamped with an official Department of Justice purple

seal, that listed — on the basis of the block and plot numbers I
had provided — the owners' names, dates of transactions,
metrage, property divisions, and boundaries as of March 31,
1945, when the last official activity was noted, as well as the
book (#1015) and page numbers (p. 8123) of the volumes Spry
had rescued. The British data had been translated into Hebrew
and computerized since then, and in this process a few typos
seemed to have been tossed into the already-dizzying brew. In
the earliest notation there, the owner had for some reason transferred information about the house from one Ottoman registry
book to another. This must have occurred on July 1, 1917, but
it was listed as 1317, an obvious impossibility since the Turks
did not arrive in Palestine for another two hundred years and,
anyhow, the land that would one day be Musrara was at the
time, and until 1870 — when a few intrepid families swallowed
their fear of roving bandits and lions and began to venture out
beyond the crowded confines of the Old City walls — nothing
but an empty stretch of rocks. Then again, maybe this wasn't a
typist's mistake at all. Could it be that the record mixed
Gregorian dates with Muslim, lunar ones, and that 01/07/1317
was not July 1, 1317, at all, but the first day of the month of
Rajab in the 1,317th year of the Hejira — that is, 1901 on the
calendar the British authorities would have recognized?

What, though, beyond the dates and names, did these nota-
tions mean? I could not decipher all the codes myself, and so
brought them to a lawyer, R., a close friend's new boyfriend,
who worked at a research institute in a stone mansion in a
quiet, ritzy part of town. This house, too, he told me, had its
history: built by "Jewish Arabs," members of Jerusalem's long-
standing community of Sephardic aristocrats at the turn of the
century. In one apartment downstairs — R. hadn't seen it himself, though he'd heard — the original bathroom still stood,
with its sunken marble tub and elegant old brass fixtures.

He surveyed the papers I placed before him and tried, piece by piece, to understand and explain them. It was, he admitted, difficult, even impossible on the basis of this particular document to say anything for certain: The records were impartial, filled with odd holes and gray patches, with some crucial information missing entirely. (The Ministry of Justice had itself added a disclaimer, declaring the registration of the property in question "NOT IN ORDER.") One man, Hajj Hassan Ben Halil Al _____, was listed as an owner as far back as that 1917/1317/1901 date, though his portion of the property only constituted two-thirds of the whole. To whom had the rest belonged? And where, too, were the lines drawn within the house? Were the rooms that would one day make up our apartment a part of Hajj Hassan's quarters at all, or did they belong to that other, shadow figure? What was the nature of the transaction that took place in March 1945, when three men with the same (Muslim) last name acquired equal parts of the house? It looked, on the face of it, like an inheritance, though the word *sale* appeared here, without further explanation. Who were these men? From whom had they purchased their share of the house? Collectively, their portion amounted to that earlier, missing third: Did Hajj Hassan still hold the rights to the rest, alongside them, or had he sold them a segment of what he owned? If so, who held the deed to the rest of the house?

Were these men brothers going in on a joint business venture? A father and his two sons? And what had happened three years later, after the departure of the British and the war, when the cease-fire line had been drawn just two streets away and this house come under Israeli control? Where were the three men then? According to the law, if they were not physically present in the house on September 1, 1948, the place could automatically be seized by the so-called Custodian of Absentee Properties. I had read accounts of how, by the end of May

1949, the neighborhood had already been settled by new immigrants. Still, even if the houses had become the de facto homes
of Jewish families, why hadn't de jure measures been taken to
mark this change in the books?

"This is just the tip of the iceberg," announced R., who had
cheerfully begun to draw up a list for me of possible sources for
further information. There were, he said, ways to fill in at least
some of these blanks. I'd need to look in certain files, which
meant I would first have to get power of attorney from X, and
then I could also consult with Y, who might be able to provide
more precise material, which would in turn lead me to Z. He
was being kind and lawyerly, as I had hoped that he would be,
but even as he spoke, I could feel my grip on the hard facts I'd
been so eager to locate slipping, giving way to another state of
mind altogether, and one I couldn't very well admit to R., who
had after all just Xeroxed my documents and offered to consult
with the institute's expert on such matters, and to look for an
article he knew of, that might provide historical data on the
process of land expropriation, and . . .

I was swept suddenly by a longing to be done forever with
this wild goose chase. This feeling was born in part of fatigue
— what I'd thought was the end of a long and complicated
search was in truth just a beginning — as well as a plainer
recognition of the self-serving and potentially cruel nature of
the task I had set myself, and by inadvertent extension the
Palestinians who had once lived in the house. It was not that I
wasn't curious to learn more, just that in discovering the identity of our apartment's former owners, I still hadn't come close
to *knowing* anything at all. And to know, in the tactile (not the
legal) terms that would matter to me, would mean to track
down these people or their descendants and pry, ask them
dozens of questions about their memories of life in the house.
Meanwhile, the cost of exacting such information, about their

furniture, food, neighbors, musical tastes, might well exceed the value of my quest. Who did I think I was? Why did I think they should want to reveal these particulars to me? What three-thousand-year-old mess was I getting myself into? Though of course by merely coming to live here I was already involved. . . . "Very deep is the well of the past." Thomas Mann got it right: "Should we not call it bottomless?"

With my earlier doubts only magnified and my findings officially "NOT IN ORDER," I decided to stop. There were, I saw now, details better left vague or buried, their sharp, bony edges allowed to dull with the years — to rest in peace, as it were. Peace *might* come, and with it an overarching resolution to at least some of this conflict — but my digging wasn't going to help it along.

><>◇><

Olive oil was hard to come by that season. Because of the hot summer, I'd been told, the olive harvest was tiny. Families were keeping and pressing or curing what they'd gathered for themselves.

"*Zeit?*" It was one of my only Arabic words, from *zeitun,* "olives," *zeitim* in Hebrew, and I uttered it now, after crossing the highway and passing the 4 Eyes optical clinic, the Al Amin and Mussrarah bakeries, with their heaps of sesame-covered cookies, meat pies, and pastel-frosted cakes on display. "Oil?" the old man in the grocery store squinted at me, sizing me up in the Friday-evening half dark, and reached behind him for the pale unctuous stuff my foreign demeanor must have suggested, a large plastic bottle of synthetic-looking, yellowish sunflower essence. "*La,*" I tried. "No. *Zeit Zeitun.*" It seemed redundant, but was apparently necessary to explain I meant *olive* oil. In Arabic, as in English (whose *oil* comes from the Greek *elaia,* "olive"), the root of the word had by now been watered down and had floated away on a generic, mass-produced slick of soy and corn.

"*La,*" he bounced back at me in Arabic then finished in Hebrew, as he turned away. "I have none."

At the next stand, with its mishmash of traditional and new-fangled goods — the shelves of *tehina,* rose and orange blossom water, open sacks of rice, beans, birdseed, and dried-yogurt balls alongside the economy-sized Pampers packages, sliced white bread, potato chips, and piles of soda and sugar syrup bottles whose contents came in the craziest make-believe colors — turquoise, bright orange, and lollipop red — I asked again "*Zeit zeitun?*" and the man shook his head no without saying a word.

But at the last shop along this stretch, whose merchandise consisted of another crowded patchwork array of old-styled and new goods, wares both organic and completely artificial, a young man with serious spectacles nodded at my request, waved me inside, and called out something in Arabic to his father or uncle, behind the counter. The older man gave me the same thoughtful nod, then disappeared behind a wall of high-stacked cans, finally producing a single, tall, shapely plastic Coca-Cola bottle, its label still intact, cleaned and filled to the top with the grassy green oil I'd been searching for, a kind of liquid treasure. Feeling lucky, I paid, thanked them both and, clutching my prize, turned and ambled westward. Night was falling fast as I passed back out of that other city, across the highway, over one street, and up one more, alongside the ever staring wall of windows.

WHAT IS THIS?

ⓍⓍⓍⓍⓍⓍⓍⓍⓍⓍⓍⓍⓍⓍⓍⓍⓍⓍⓍⓍⓍ

whenever amram was in, he left his door ajar — whether out of habit or as a sign to us that he was well I do not know. He had various health problems and an enormous belly, which he would bare throughout the summer as he sat alone in his green gym shorts watching soccer or TV movies. Just across the hallway we shared, his apart-ment was actually a single large room, sparsely furnished and dotted with several old framed pictures of a rabbi, his own late mother, and himself as a glowering young Rabat brute, his then-narrow face softened somewhat by a greased cowlick and bisected by a thin black mustache that looked painted on. Besides his bad heart, he had trouble with his eyes and for some time after an operation shed nonstop croc-odile tears, which he hid behind a buggish set of pink plastic women's sunglasses when he ventured out into the bright light

— a vision so disturbing the first time I saw it, I could only respond by gesturing for him to lean down and let me peel off the price tag from the middle of one lens. He did so with sheepish obedience and then thanked me by means of a wordless little grunt before he plodded off, his cheeks still streaked with tears.

He slept on the couch, kept the entirety of his modest belongings in a few standing closets, and did his cooking on a camp stove in the tight corridor of a kitchen in the back. His diet consisted mostly of fried frozen fish, according to the smells that wafted into our own apartment, along with the airborne savor of the dozens of artichokes or multiple kilos of green beans that he would, in their respective seasons, lug home in large plastic bags from the *shuk* and boil all at once, to eat throughout the week. He had no hot water and, when we first moved in, no phone, though in time he made this small concession to the neighborhood's modernization. Still, it rang very rarely, maybe once every two weeks. His family was made up of a bevy of sisters and brothers and their children and grandchildren, with whom he dutifully passed the holidays and an occasional Shabbat. When he needed to speak to us he would usually just tap on the door, open it, then step into our apartment, his gigantic bare belly clearing space before him like a late-term pregnancy. But on those weekends when he took the bus to go visit his relatives in Beer Sheva, he would tell us he was going by knocking with a formal *rat-a-tat-tat,* then greeting me with the familiar diminutive that he understood was my name in full, "*Shalom,* Dina." His suddenly decorous demeanor was apparently inspired by the shower, shave, and clean cotton shirt he'd affected for the occasion. Perhaps he wanted to show off. He was well past sixty years old and had lived alone, taken care of himself for decades now, and yet, as he stood there in the front hall, his gray hair neatly combed, knitted skullcap planted on his bald spot, one fist clutching a bit anxiously at the handle of the little plaid suitcase he had packed for the weekend, he always seemed to me a small boy, nervous at having to travel alone. And I, despite myself, would be swept by what I imagine to be an almost maternal wistfulness at sending him off unprotected into the unknown.

He had never married. Grumbled reference was made to his one true love, a canceled engagement some forty-five years before, and his broken heart, though he also made it plain that he had grown to prefer — in fact *enjoy* — his autonomy to any other still-feasible arrangement. He would often cut those family visits short and come whizzing home on the very first bus after the Saturday-night dark was official and it was kosher to travel.

One sister in Marseilles, he said, had invited him to come live with her, offering him a room in her house, but he had refused her out of hand. *This* place was his home, his corner in the world, his life. (He assumed an indignant tone as he made this declaration.) He'd made do well enough in the same room for the last forty-eight years, hadn't he, watching and listening as dozens of people clattered through the house and past his windows — noisy young families, loudmouthed patriarchs, shrill grandmothers, delinquents, whores, junkies, gentrifiers, journalists, the drunken kook who once lived in what was now our apartment and who had spent every night, according to Amram, delivering fiery political addresses to a room full of empty bottles. (For some time, a group of rowdy teenagers thought it hilarious to stand at the window and hoot prime ministers' names in ghoulish tones, to spook the old lush, but Amram had chased the good-for-nothing punks away.) And he remained now, a kind of survivor, one who did not take his long-awaited privacy lightly or for granted. When he first came to this country, the building was a sort of welfare dormitory for single men, and he'd lived in this same room with three or four others, an experience he described with a nearly nostalgic strain of gallows humor: Once, he rhapsodized sardonically, he came home after a few days out of town to find the guy in the next cot, a Romanian, dead. (He knew by the smell.) Another time, when there was no work, he and his roommates had gone for a whole month eating nothing but bread. With the years, the others left,

one at a time or a few together, due to marriage, illness, con-
scription, lodging or work found elsewhere, emigration, lack of
funds, a sudden windfall, and he stayed on, till at last he was the
sole remaining boarder.

Then the dormitory closed for good and Amram arranged to
pay a pittance in key money to call the room his own. After all
that, he certainly wasn't about to give up and slink off to
Marseilles, or around the block for that matter. *No thank you.*
No one would tell him what to eat, when to sleep, when to
shower, and — despite the incorrigible neighborhood meddlers,
who would mutter at what a *mizken,* a poor thing, he was to live
alone, to fend for himself all these years; *He has no wife, he has
no children,* they would shake their heads and condescend in a
buzzardlike chorus — there was something quietly heroic about
Amram's independence. I cannot, of course, know if he'd chosen
this way of life, though if he was suffering in his solitude, he
showed no obvious signs. I had a strong hunch that he was
telling the truth when he defended with defiance "his life" and
all the minute daily choices that this term entailed. And why
not? He knew his own needs and likes better than anyone. He
watched the soccer games till late at night, working his way in
rabbitlike contentment through a paper bag filled with sunflower seeds, played his favorite radio station when he swept the
floor on Friday mornings, and sometimes prepared himself a
special feast. One day we smelled something burning at midday
and knocked at his half-open door to be sure nothing was wrong
— *Amram? Everything all right?* On hearing our knocks and
calls, he emerged bare-bellied and triumphant from his tiny back
courtyard, spatula in hand: He was cooking himself some liver
on the barbecue, he said, through a sloped half smile and mouth
full of food. *Nothing's burning. That's my lunch.*

We were not being overly cautious. Once Amram's room *had*
been threatened by fire, and we had no desire to see that dismal

scene repeated. It was late afternoon and I was alone in our apartment, washing the dishes with distracted movements as I mused. I did not hear the sounds at first, so accustomed had I become to blocking out the children's calls and workers' clatter from the street. It took at least ten minutes, in fact, and the advent of a strong acrid smell for me to realize that something was indeed very wrong and that a low but steady groan was seeping from a place nearby — from Amram's apartment just a few feet away, or was it from the front hallway . . . ?

I rushed to open our door and found the entry filled with thickening gray smoke and Amram slumped along one wall. He clutched a burn on his arm, squeezed his eyes shut, and whimpered softly as a wounded animal. Beside him, his apartment door hung open and the noxious scent was pouring steadily toward us. The front door was locked from the inside and by now a few other neighbors had begun to pound from the street, in the hope that someone inside would hear and open up. I scrambled for the key, let them in, and ran to call the fire department, which soon arrived. The flames turned out to be more minor than they first had seemed: His cooking-gas cannister had exploded and blackened the wall and table nearby but otherwise caused little damage, injuring him just slightly. But no matter that the actual harm was negligible, the effect had been dramatic, and only after the trucks had pulled away, the other neighbors begun to disperse, and the scent of dampened soot turned to a sweet and mocking perfume did I find that I was shaking. Amram continued to slouch but had relocated to a safer spot across the street, and as I heaved myself down on the stoop beside him, I saw that he was also shivering and that his eyes, though now open, were still clouded with fear — as if he'd seen his own death brush up against him and then for some reason move on, leaving him here to breathe heavily and tremble as he cradled the reddened patch on his arm. From his war stories, the several heart attacks he had suffered in the last few years, and the stunned expression he wore on the day he staggered home from the *shuk* after missing a terrorist's bomb by a few hundred yards, I knew this was not the first time that his mortality had come to call then turned and walked away.

He had, he'd once twisted to show me, with his typically undiluted blend of gruff pride, testy anger, and childlike shyness, shrapnel from the Sinai Campaign still lodged in the back of his neck. When he had at last come home, bandaged, from the field hospital in '56, the whole neighborhood was stunned: The army had listed him among the dead and now here he was, walking toward them! He had risen! He liked this story and would tell it often, obviously pleased to think how the premature report of his demise had made his sisters weep. Maybe one day he would also laugh at the tale of this cooking fire, but as we sat in silence, side by side, recovering from the sudden frenzy and the just-as-sudden denouement the past hour had brought, Amram looked utterly spent, as if he knew that by now he'd almost exhausted his stockpile of heavenly reprieves and couldn't manage too many times more to avoid his own grand finale — the real and irreversible one, whose outline could never be repeated as amusing anecdote. . . . Thinking back, it seems that what scared me most that day, what made my teeth rattle and pulse pound in my ears, was not the fire itself, but the image of this heavy-shouldered, self-sufficient lug of a man reduced to wailing faintly in the front hallway as he prepared himself to die. For that split second, Amram did seem to me alone — terribly alone and as vulnerable as anyone could be. If I'd moved to act efficiently, without panicking, it seems to me in retrospect not bravery but a kind of cowardice, acute embarrassment at seeing him so helpless and exposed.

Most of our interactions with Amram were hardly so existential: We learned to allow each other as wide a berth as possible, given our very close quarters. Sometimes we wouldn't see his face once for a few days running, but would register his presence almost unconsciously, according to the sight of his partly opened door and to a familiar sequence of sounds — of his radio or TV set, of hissing oil in his one frying pan, of his wooden door clicking closed in its frame, followed immediately by the soft jangle of keys turning in his lock, of his halting footsteps and the prayer he mumbled upon leaving the house each morning. Mishmish, our sensitive tomcat, took this instinctive awareness one step farther, and could distinguish the sound of Amram's door keys from our own, even from the street. If I were in the apartment alone and Peter's key turned in the front lock, the cat would wrest himself from the heaviest, most tightly wound slumber to go greet the newcomer with a luxuriant little roll at his feet; if it was Amram, he knew, without fail, to snooze on.

One year, after we canceled our cable TV subscription — thereby rendering our set nothing more than a VCR screen, since without this rented service there was no reception in our house, locked as we were into the hill's slope — I happened upon Amram at his post before Mani's mini-market, where he rested under the awning on warm-weather afternoons. This was part of the fixed if considerably slowed-down schedule he insisted on maintaining at least a decade past retirement from his construction job: He shuffled in the morning to the community center to sit at the "club" there, with the other old people, after which he would lumber home for lunch, then move onto Mani's, where for several hours he would occupy a white plastic chair, suck Popsicles, and talk with the bleary-looking shop owner and other passersby, his mouth gone purple or blue from the flavor of the day. If Mani was occupied inside and the customers were few, Amram seemed content to tilt his head toward his chest, fold his hands before him, and rest in patient silence.

Although this lounging spot was just a few blocks from our house, he would greet me when I came to shop there with the hearty, slightly startled *Hello-and-how-are-you* one might save for an old friend encountered after years and by chance on a busy street in a far-off country.

On this particular afternoon, our conversation turned to the inevitable subject of the ongoing World Cup. His face lit up at the suggestion that Peter might even consider missing the Game, whichever the Game was that day. *"You don't have television?"* he asked, incredulous. (He himself had agreed to pay the steep cable fees even before he conceded to telephone installation.) "Then he'll watch with me! We'll drink coffee! We'll eat watermelon! He should come!" Peter himself had been reluctant to ask. "Maybe he *wants* to watch alone," he said, but I doubted it — I could tell from the tenor of Amram's greeting when he was feeling lonely. If he called out *"Shalom,* Dina!" before I greeted him, I could see he wanted company and would linger a few extra minutes near the front of the store, making formulaic but affectionate small talk. And so it was arranged: Peter went, they watched, and at halftime he was treated to a spontaneous photography exhibit, an array of snapshots of his host as teenage Moroccan bruiser, kicking a soccer ball across an open lot. "Now," Amram explained importantly, "the *king* is buried under that field. They have guards around his tomb. Guards with guns!" I was nearly asleep when Peter returned to our side of the foyer, bearing a gift from Amram to us — his old, free-standing antenna that should, our neighbor promised, bring us at least partial reception. Peter said he was insistent, almost scandalized at the thought that we were living in such a state of technological deprivation. "How else can you pass the hours?"

Another time, our upstairs neighbor, Ezra, the widower whose wife had been killed in a terrorist carjacking, neglected to pay our joint water bill for so long that the municipality removed the meter and cut our pipes off from the main. The moment the flow in our faucet vanished to a trickle and then stopped, I knew what had happened. We'd been hassling Ezra for months to settle his — and by extension our — growing debt, at which he would blush and look askance and promise to pay up tomorrow, translated loosely as meaning "not now." But to be sure I crossed the hallway to check with Amram and see if by some fluke he still had water. He did not.

"WHAT IS THIS?" he roared, in an early-morning slur, after checking his own dried-out spigot. "WHAT?"

It was a good question. After mounting the staircase to Ezra's and finding no one there but the two little boys and the noisy pacifier of a TV cartoon I realized I had no choice but to give up a workday, take our own checkbook, and venture out toward City Hall myself, in the hope of restoring our water supply sometime before next week. "I'm coming too," announced Amram, his tone stubborn and brow knotted darkly. And then he gurgled again, to himself this time: *What is this?* He continued to mumble and curse as we walked side by side the short uphill distance to City Hall. We must have cut quite a figure, the slight young woman with the Western stride and leather pocketbook and the towering older Moroccan man in his skullcap and sandals, wiping sweat from his forehead as he muttered to himself, circling compulsively around a few choice phrases. *"What kind of a man is that? What kind of father? Doesn't pay his bills . . . bastard. What is this? Who does he think he is?"* The longer he went on in this agitated vein, the more convinced he seemed to grow of the personal nature of Ezra's offense — as if our neighbor's failure to pay the water bill were intended as conscious insult to Amram himself. He didn't spare me his self-pity, and grew angrier the farther we walked. *"I'm a simple man. I don't have many needs. Just simple things. A roof, a bed, some food, a shower — but I can't take a shower today. We don't have water! That son of a bitch didn't pay the bill! What is this, no water? What?"* and so forth.

In some detached way I recognized the hilarity of our joint march on City Hall. But the depressing prospect of the hassles before us was enough to keep me sober. As we progressed from desk to desk, relating our predicament to a long line of indifferent bureaucrats (each of whom would listen blankly then direct us with a passive shrug to another department on another floor), it grew harder to keep a straight face — though as always in such cases the question of whether to laugh or to cry was a good one. In each instance, I would begin a bit timidly in the careful Hebrew sentences I'd rehearsed in my head before speaking, and each time, midway through my explanation, Amram would bellow at the top of his lungs. "WHAT IS THIS? THEY TURNED OFF OUR WATER! WE HAVE NO WATER! THIEVES!" Neither strategy worked very well, since the clerks continued to send us elsewhere, down newly carpeted, fluorescent-lit hallways and into crowded elevators. All this traipsing was rough on Amram and at a certain point, after we'd descended to the labyrinth of the basement and been told to ask at yet another office down yet another corridor, I could see that he was in pain. His breathing had become labored, he was sweating profusely and had stopped his muttering. "Are you okay, Amram?" I asked him, nervous that the strain of the morning might bring on another heart attack. "Why don't you go back home? I can finish this myself. . . ."

"No." He took a heavy breath and leaned for a minute against the wall then, pulling himself to stand upright again, issued an elephantine groan and ordered me firmly, "Come on." So on we walked, eventually arriving in a large office where all the city's confiscated water meters were arrayed across folding tables as if for inspection. That did it: The actual, physical proximity of our own meter gave Amram enough strength to bellow once more, even more loudly than before: "GIVE US OUR METER! YOU TOOK OUR METER! CROOKS!" At this, the cold-eyed clerk stared at Amram with undisguised European contempt and ordered "the gentleman" to lower his voice. The man cast a pitying look at me, then through a pinched little sneer arranged for us to receive our meter later that same day. As I limped off alone to go pay the cashier, I thought it fortunate that Amram had come along that day. Although I could write a check to cover our bill, I could never have blustered with his no-holds-barred conviction. It seems that the clerk had acted with such haughty dispatch not because he was persuaded by Amram but simply to shut him up. This rude slap of a fact might have offended or mortified another, but not Amram, who had long ago put basic needs above etiquette and was clearly accustomed — to the point of obliviousness — to the absorption of insults.

Which didn't mean he lacked pride. Later that evening, when our water finally sputtered back on, he knocked at our door to ask, "Okay?" and perhaps to gloat just a bit at having played a lead role in its restoration.

"Okay," I assured him.

"Me too," he announced loftily, then exhaled his weary good-night and shuffled the three steps home.

><><><

Without ever admitting that he could not read, Amram used his brusque manner well, to get us to explain his mail. The invitation he received to Ezra's wedding was no exception. "What is this?" He demanded to know, irritated. "What?" he thrust the pink, daisy-and-butterfly-strewn card before him in the same heated way he would push a phone bill or Social Security statement at one of us and ask with annoyance, "What do they want from me?"

We had also been invited to the big event, Ezra's mid-June nuptials to his much-younger girlfriend, to be held at a banquet hall in the city's industrial zone, the location of choice for such affairs. When Amram heard what was printed on the card he relaxed, grinned, and patted his stomach, as if in hungry anticipation of the many courses of the wedding feast. "We'll go together," he declared, not one to bear a grudge over water bills now long since paid. "We'll take a taxi. We'll do this the *right* way." We agreed, and on the day of the wedding, fifteen minutes before the ceremony was due to start, I tapped lightly on his door.

"Amram? I'm going to call a taxi now."

"Now?" The soccer game blasted from his TV set and he sat, still barefoot, wearing nothing but his green gym shorts. "It's early," he assured me. "No one gets there on time." Unsure, I retreated to our own apartment and waited another quarter hour or so before I went ahead and called.

"Amram? I called," I announced, and heard a loud sigh from inside his room.

A few minutes later he emerged in a clean shirt and pants and as the three of us moved to the corner to await the cab, Amram grumbled, shaking his head. "We'll be the first ones there, you'll see."

After a rather farcical ride in which Amram and the driver parried boisterously and exchanged a cheerful battery of insults ("How long have you been driving a cab and you don't know where _____ is?" "Longer than you've been driving a cab!"), we wound up circling around and around the designated block, in search of the right banquet hall. There were dozens along this particular stretch and as it turned out, the name on our invitation was a misprint. Eventually we found the right building and Amram pulled a wad of cash from his pocket, adamant that we let him pay for the taxi. By now, his tone had developed a sweetly avuncular edge, as it seemed to have occurred to him that all the book learning in the world — our ability to speak English and decipher the fine print on his Hebrew pension check — would not help get us through the evening ahead. On the subject of How to Be a Guest at a Big Moroccan Wedding, he was the authority, we the illiterates, and as he swept out of the taxi — "Come!" he gestured grandly — it was plain he'd decided to act as both our valet and host, take us under his wing, guide his innocent young American friends with gentle patience and force through all the wonders he knew the evening held in store.

As we made our way past the dimly lit sign and into the shabby foyer, with its peeling paint and battered elevator, it was clear that he'd been right on at least the first score: Although we were technically half an hour late we were still very early, some of the first guests to show. A few of the bride's older brothers smoked outside and a group of little boys in white shirts and sneakers were racing up and down the stairs. Otherwise the only other arrivals were several stragglers like us and the parents of the bride and groom, waiting uncomfortably to receive guests. The two women wore low-cut, sequined evening gowns and heavy costume jewelry, as well as high spike heels that made them seem taller than their husbands, both of whom looked fairly miserable in their baggy new suits. Ezra's children and their friends had just made their entrance. The girls held hands and compared mini-dresses and the boys played a loud game of tag. Meanwhile, long before most of the guests had appeared, a battalion of teenage waiters and waitresses in red vests and black bow ties were already distractedly distributing their large trays of pickles, salads, *pitot,* and sweet wine across the strangely floating, shiplike expanse of a banquet hall.

A forest of mirror-covered pillars interrupted the vast room, the entire second floor of a building, which was filled with dozens and dozens of identically set tables and gold-gift-ribbon-wrapped chairs. The low but endless-looking ceiling flashed a full constellation of tiny colored lights, and although the white satin bridal canopy rested atop a small flight of stairs at the end of a theatrical strip of red carpet — thus forming the would-be centerpiece of the entire hall and evening — it seemed to me that in fact the true source of the room's insistent sparkle, its hideous, fascinating glow, was not this token religious object but the huge glass sun of a disco ball that hung and winked from above. An electric guitar player with long, pomaded curls and a shiny tux was testing the amplifiers while American pop music trickled faintly over the loudspeakers, interrupted by an occasional, abrupt snort of feedback from the stage. Although the hall was still mostly empty, a ponytailed barmaid stood near the entrance, rattling her little pushcart with its rows of salted shot glasses and a silver-capped bottle. "Tequila, tequila," she called in singsong, as if at a boozy ballgame.

As we took in this typical yet astounding scene, Amram declared it was time for a drink and insisted with unusual cheer that he bring us our choice from the bar. "What will you have, Dina?" He gestured for us to sit. "Visky?"

"Vodka," I said, and soon found myself, glass in hand, ensconced at the table Amram had selected, the surface before me already arrayed with more than half a dozen small plates of food.

"Eat, Dina!" he ordered, beaming over his Jim Beam. "Petter! Eat! What's the matter with you two? What? You're not hungry?" He reached for a fried meat pastry and I knew I should do the same. Though I'd heard all the jokes about the way the plates clatter, tongues wag, and cola sloshes right through the sideshow ceremony at the average Israeli wedding — known in Hebrew as a "quarter-chicken" affair, because of the standard, uninspired menu — this hardly seemed the time to start playing Miss Manners. Our host had just suggested that we eat, so we would eat. This was Amram's party now. He looked ecstatic as he chewed and explained that he only drank whiskey at such events. With his heart, of course, it wasn't a good idea — but for a wedding? What could he do? Drink! *L'chaim!* (Early on, I noticed that one young waiter seemed to have appointed himself our personal attendant, standing close by at all times, waiting to replenish a dwindling pile of bourekas or plate of cabbage salad. Only later did Peter nudge me to look as Amram peeled a large bill from his wad and handed it to the boy, as he'd apparently been doing throughout the evening.) After another glass or two, he began to whisper about Ezra's first, murdered wife, and indicated, with a conspiratorial little roll of the hand before his own bursting belly, that Ezra's second wife-to-be was already visibly pregnant.

Bit by bit, other guests filtered in — I recognized very few of them — and our table became the assembly point for a peculiar array of misfits, ourselves most definitely included. First there was Shlomi, the jumpy soccer fan and hummus-joint waiter who lived across the street and remained dangerously in awe of Peter's gardening skills. (That is, the more he appreciated the fruit trees, roses, and jasmine that Peter had planted and tended with such care, the greater the threat he would try and "help out" by paving the courtyard with cement blocks.) "What's happening?" he asked us all as he sat down and in the same movement reached for a plate of *tehina* salad. Then, mouth full, "What do you say, Amram?" Naturally, he'd waited to come till the Game was over, and so spent the next ten minutes rehashing for Amram in thick monotone a complete and numbing play-by-play.

Then in came Mani, the neighborhood's lesser grocer, minus his wife and children. He looked worn (up since five, he announced with a yawn) and flopped in the seat beside me, cigarette in hand. Although he still was no match for Meir-the-master, his own shopkeeping skills had improved immeasurably of late. He was more confident, friendlier, and the merchandise on his shelves seemed to reflect his new-and-improved outlook: He kept it fresh and varied, and had even begun stocking items that Meir himself didn't have, such as parsley and tonic water. I'd had a few silly, heated discussions with my best college friend, Lauren, who had recently moved right next door to Mani's store and who went so far as to insist that *he* and not Meir commanded the best mini-market for miles. . . . It was, admittedly, a stupid subject for an argument (roughly on an intellectual par with our ongoing, reductive debate about the relative beauty and intelligence of dogs, which she claimed were superior creatures, and cats, my own animal of choice), but we each clung so fiercely to our partisan beliefs that we had, in the end, to call it a draw and admit that the two blocks that separated our apartments might have seemed scant from a distance but in fact constituted an ocean of perspective-altering difference. In effect, we lived in separate neighborhoods, each with its own local heroes.

Even so, as Mani sat down beside me, I felt my old critique of him peeking out like a crooked slip from under my hem. And now I was obliged to make small talk. How was business? How were his kids? He seemed slightly amused to find us at this wedding, and when I'd run through the usual list of personal–impersonal topics for chatter, I asked him if he had grown up in the neighborhood, where was his childhood house, what was it like to live by the border. He answered a few of my questions in an opaque and mechanical way, then locked me with a knowing stare and informed me, through a puff of indifferent smoke (getting even at last for my preference in grocers?), that I was writing a book. Busted, I gulped hard and took a big swig of my vodka. Yes, I was, in fact. How had he known? He smiled only faintly and shrugged, not particularly interested. *I just knew.*

By now the hall was crowded, the dishes were indeed clinking on all sides, and the music had grown louder. At the back of the room, a voluminous wedding dress and dark mound of sprayed curls were visible, though the bride's face was obscured by a crowd of spangled and stiletto-heeled well-wishers. Our other upstairs neighbors slipped in at this point and seemed relieved to find us there. He was a charming cynic of an Italian journalist whose native-sounding American English came from a New York childhood, his immaculate wardrobe from Rome, and she, his girlfriend, a gregarious Australian divorcée with coiffed blond hair and ambassadorial social skills. A few years after we moved into our apartment, they'd bought half the top floor of the building and set to thundering work raising the roof and turning the inside of their apartment into a luxurious two-story penthouse — at once defacing the outside of the structure with a few rows of new stone and, ironically enough, bringing the house back around full circle to its original function, as spacious home of the well-off. Though we were unhappy with what they had done to the house's facade, we couldn't very well blame them for it, since they knew well what an irreversible and costly mess they had made and were furious at their contractor. After the initial tensions between us were defused, we'd grown to be friends of a formal but gradually warming sort, kindred spirits drawn closer by the trials of living in the neighborhood . . . by the band of beefy, sneering teenagers, for instance, who would lounge on the corner and see if they could get a rise out of one of us by muttering "Ashke-Nazi" as we walked by, or by Shlomi-the-soccer-fan's decision to hire someone — "my Romanian," as he called the worker who had lately replaced "my Arab" — to cut down the quartet of old cypresses that stood above Ahmed's garden (in Ahmed's absence: He had never returned). Peter had at least managed to intervene and convince him that only one, long dead, required chopping down, and that perhaps a tree surgeon might be better equipped to do the job. But this wasn't enough to stop Shlomi, who still wanted to *do* something. In a fit of destructive busy-ness, he proceeded to get "his" Romanian drunk, and sent him up another trunk, to hack a bit. Alarmed to see a soused stranger hard at work mangling the view out his window, Carl called downstairs to ask what was going on. Peter explained, and in a moment of the peculiar intimacy that shared disaster can bring, the two of them stood — weary, disgusted, tele-phones in hand — looking out from their respective floors.

We had also exchanged invitations for dinner and drinks with Carl and Sylvia. They had come downstairs to chat and nibble olives on our porch and, in turn, had asked us several times to parties at their place, which was just upstairs but seemed to exist in another galaxy, on high. Most of the guests at those evening gatherings were handsome Italians, women with smooth tans and bangle bracelets, smoking and sipping imported white wine, and men who managed to look at once casual and dressed to kill in their roomy linen jackets. While the talk was always animated, its cadences were distinct from those of spirited local conversation: That it was more refined goes without saying. Its music seemed closer to that of a burbling fountain than to the geyser gusts that punctuated most Israeli speech. I do not speak Italian, but found that an evening spent listening to others do so was a comfort. And when the conver-sation was stripped of its exotic, lilting sound and gave way to broken English, I was always pleasantly surprised at the dryly fatalistic wit that tinged most of what was being said. Carl's Italian friends were knowing in an elegant, unpretentious way that few Americans ever manage, and as a group they chal-lenged my prejudice against foreign journalists. Reporting seemed to be, for many of them, a job rather than a worldview, an enterprise like any other, to be treated with a certain skeptical sense of humor. One man, with a trim mustache and a deep, caustic laugh, explained as he nursed his dwindling cigarette and swished the grappa in his glass that he much preferred newspapers but worked, for now, "in the television," about which he sighed wearily: "Is so shallow, so silly. No time to *explain* things."

Given the usual company he kept, it was no wonder that Carl looked unhappy now, surrounded by flashing lights and the outlandish hodgepodge of people at our table. We broke into English over the din, while Sylvia eased herself into the incredible situation with her usual steady grace — offering her most serene smile as she greeted all the members of our group individually and by name, in the appropriate language. (Of the some five hundred guests, the four of us were probably the only Ashkenazis and the only foreigners there, a fact that seemed to me glaring, though I doubt that anyone else even noticed.) Carl relaxed a bit when our zealous waiter scrambled to find him a carafe of cold wine and we silently toasted.

It was time for the ceremony to begin. The American pop halted, the music modulated to a more stately key, and the bride began to mince down the carpet, mother and mother-in-law-to-be stationed on either arm. Whether or not she was truly pregnant was difficult to tell, since the overall effect of her elaborately "sexy" costume was a total negation of body and skin: She'd been tied, pushed, wrapped, and buttoned so thoroughly into her corset and frothy meringue of synthetic skirting, I couldn't say for sure who — or what — was in there. Even later, when the veil came off and she removed the little lace bolero she'd worn over her bare shoulders to satisfy the rabbi, I wasn't sure what she really looked like, or even if I had ever seen her before. Her face was covered with several layers of makeup so thick, it was unclear if she was blushing or blanched. She appeared to be embalmed.

Ezra, for his part, seemed nervous and hot as he stood beneath the *chuppa,* wiping his brow almost constantly. I wondered if the sweating came from the bright lights that shined down all around him (the photographer and video cameraman were already hard at work, snapping and circling for a better angle) or from an unfathomable set of fears and hesitations. Except when her name was whispered by Amram and then brushed away (bad luck), and probably muttered at other tables, in the same fleet hush, Ezra's first wife wasn't mentioned throughout the whole evening, though her memory couldn't possibly be absent — not from Ezra's mind, nor his parents' nor children's nor friends'. And what of the bride's awareness of the much-loved first wife and her violent end? Later, when the slippery emcee invited the newlyweds onto the floor for their first married dance (to the theme from *Titanic,* which struck me as a rather morbid way to kick off a life together), he referred to them compulsively as "the young couple." Did it sting Ezra, this generic, inaccurate term, the thoughtless public erasure of his first wife's memory? Or did it come as a relief? *Young,* of course, was a relative term, and Ezra *was* young for a man with four children, two of whom were his new wife's junior by just a few crucial years. Still, in this context *young* also implied a kind of innocence that Ezra could no longer claim.

As expected, most of the guests ate right through the ceremony and clapped when Ezra smashed the glass with his foot — a rite that symbolized at one and the same time the end of the ritual, the start of the marriage, the destruction of the Temple, and the cue for the waiters to bring out the main course. Out it came, and round and round: Amram signaled his attendant to bring ours speedily and he obliged, spreading before us another impressive, exhausting array of meat, chicken, fish, vegetables, rice, and even a towering plate of fried brains that Amram insisted I try. He dug in to set an example.

A belly dancer appeared now, her distant half smile apparently part of the show, and began to shimmy for the newlyweds, inviting the bride to wiggle along with her, eye to eye. And wiggle she did, her arms raised in a loose but snakelike manner, hips and breasts swinging in apparent freedom yet in fact (the longer I watched, the more I understood) confined to tracing a fixed swishing pattern. . . . By then the musicians had recalibrated and switched to a syncopated Eastern beat as the bride and the belly dancer, gazes locked, jiggled together out onto the floor, in a ritual crackling with both the charge of seduction and contest. Shosh, the bride, was a fine dancer and a good sport, though as the evening went on and the whole hall joined in the gyrations, I saw the bizarre power of this dancing to turn the least attractive women, their skin haggard, hair thinned by dye and age, stomachs stretched from frequent childbirth, into almost purely sexual creatures — not in a vulgar way, but through the sly sort of understatement that infected even the most loudly dressed and rowdy of them as they wordlessly twisted their hips. The women danced with one another, their arms curved above their heads, never touching but coordinating their movements and keeping close. And they all wore a similar expression of dreamy pleasure at their bodies (*vanity* is too strong a word). Each held herself as if she were the bride, the queen, the most beautiful one in the hall.

We watched and ate, and after a while the copious amounts of food and booze we'd ingested had begun to weigh down and slow the talk and laughter. Amram was a bit drunk, but in a gentle, interior way. His earlier effusive bearing had evolved by now into a more taciturn aspect, and turned him back in on his own thoughts. Peter and I considered getting up to dance — *go, dance, dance,* Amram encouraged us muddily, as if he were talking to himself — and finding ourselves in the middle of these packs of wiggling women, we danced together the only way we knew how, hand in hand, with our usual Occidental dips, twirls, and shuffles. By the time we came back to the table we were thirsty and in high spirits. Amram sat still, cryptic in his silence. Was this contentment or melancholy? His eyes scanned the room but didn't seem to see what was there. He had been to so many weddings before; this one might already, as it unfolded, be sinking into the hazily remembered pile. Would he like to dance? I asked him, and he chuckled a bit ruefully to himself. No, no. He couldn't dance any more. His heart . . .

After I deposited the requisite check and card in the designated box (to give any other gift, I'd been warned, was offensive), we started home: Carl and Sylvia offered to drive us and after we explained that we'd come with Amram, the five of us piled into their car. We spoke a muted, dinner-party English most of the way, as Amram sat, uncomprehending and hushed, docile as a weary child in the front seat. But when we arrived home, I wanted, somehow, to thank him for the evening, to finish the night in his own language, as it had begun.

"Thank you —" I started to say. "Thank you, Amram —"

"Pah." He interrupted me with a dismissive grunt. "For what? I didn't do anything."

Then he turned, smiling so faintly I couldn't be sure that he hadn't in fact grimaced, unlocked his door, and went off to sleep in his room.

CODA (FAMOUS MEN)

xxxxxxxxxxxxxxxxxxxxxxxxxxxxxxxxxxxxxxxxxxxxxx

In a novel, a house or person has his meaning, his existence, entirely through the writer. Here, a house or a person has only the most limited of his meanings through me: his true meaning is much huger. It is that he exists, in actual being, as you do and I do, and as no character of the imagination can possibly exist. His great weight, mystery, and dignity are in this fact.

James Agee
Let Us Now Praise Famous Men

amram had been ill. one morning, on the eve of the Day of Atonement, a knock came at our door and I opened it to find him standing in the front hall, his T-shirt spattered with blood. His nose was dripping the red stuff and he looked scared, standing there, asking bluntly, "Is the health clinic open today?"

It was his heart again, and after a preposterous scene in which he had to stumble out of the clinic to flag down his own ambulance (the extremely inexperienced young driver had somehow gotten lost), he was taken to the hospital, where he stayed a few days and where Peter went to see him and bring him some clothes and a razor. Amram was deeply touched — "It's like you're my son" he told my husband, in a moment of uncharacteristic expressiveness — and when he returned home he seemed seriously slowed, but grateful for our attentions, and he kept thanking us, wishing us long lives, good health . . .

"How are you, Amram? Can I get you something at the *shuk?*" At first, I tapped on his door daily, to check up on him. Later, sensing he preferred not to be fussed over, I would wait until we happened to meet in the front hall, or in the street, to ask, "How do you feel?"

And instead of the usual I'm-okay-you're-okay formula, he'd sigh in a low and total way and respond with the more honestly pessimistic: "Not so good. I'm sick. But what can I do? There's nothing to be done."

For a few weeks, we exchanged a similar, muted back-and-forth, which usually came around to the same helpless state-ment and ended with Amram painfully shuffling away . . . until one afternoon, a few days after the signing of the Wye River agreement, when Netanyahu, Arafat, Clinton, and the cancer-stricken King Hussein had gathered together for a televised cer-emony at the White House. From a distance, I saw Amram walking down the street with a bit more spring in his step than usual, and when we met I asked him: How do you feel?

"Did you see —" he started in, without answering my ques-tion, "those pictures of King Hussein? What is that?"

"What?"

"That poor man . . . He has no hair. He has no beard. *What is that?* He is the *king,* he has *palaces.* How many palaces? Three? Four? And horses, and money, all the money he could want. But," he paused for effect, and drew a wheezy breath, "but he has *nothing.* He doesn't have his health. That's all a man really needs. Without his health — he is poor, so poor he might as well be a beggar. The rest of that is worth *nothing.*"

"And how do *you* feel, Amram?" I asked again, now that we had returned to the subject.

"Me?" He looked almost confused by my question. "*I'm* fine. *I* have everything I need. I have a place to sleep, food, clothes — and my health, thank God. I've got nothing to complain about. I have all a man really needs."

Now, once again, he turned to go, but this time he did not shuffle. He walked straighter, and held his head upright, as if to balance an invisible crown. The scene was almost comic — except that Amram genuinely meant what he said, as he meant the magisterial posture he had just adopted. So I did not laugh as I watched him walk away. Instead, I straightened my own backbone, lifted my head, and silently counted my blessings.